When parents divorce, kids get hurt—there are no two ways about it. However, through understanding that you are not responsible in any way for the divorce and that hurt and angry adults are apt to behave badly at times, you can begin to adjust to the divorce. More importantly, you will be able to take the steps toward healing, and feeling secure and good again about your life.

THE KIDS' GUIDE TO DIVORCE

John P. Brogan & Ula Maiden

FAWCETT CREST • NEW YORK

A Fawcett Crest Book
Published by Ballantine Books

Library of Congress Catalog Card Number: 86-91189

ISBN: 0-449-21242-4

Manufactured in the United States of America

First Edition: December 1986

ACKNOWLEDGMENTS

John: I would like to thank my family, Marti my wife, and Mike, Pat, and Maureen for all their patience, encouragement, and understanding. I could not have written this book without their support.

Ula: I greatly thank my boys, John, David, and Eric, who have been through it. Their loyalty, honesty, and humor have helped me beyond their knowing, both in writing this book and as a person.

We wish to acknowledge all the help of those wonderful and marvelous Yorktown kids (you know who you are).

Also, Dorothy Zemper, Office of Family Life, Diocese of Toledo, Ohio; Ms. Roberta Black, Newton, Massachusetts, School District; and the Monday Night Parents Group of Yorktown.

The Board of Education and the administration of the Yorktown Central School District for the courage and determination to see "Who Gets Me for Christmas?" become an educational success.

Contents

Introduction

Each year 1.2 million children join the ranks of "divorced" kids. According to the U.S. Bureau of the Census, 12.8 million kids live with a single parent and another 7.8 million kids live in stepfamilies, most of which were formed after divorce. Incredible, isn't it? Yet when it happens to you, you feel all alone in the world and can't imagine that other kids have ever lived through anything like this.

People who deal with kids professionally recognize the problems you and others face when parents divorce. It's a very tough time for you. Some school psychologists have said that the emotional turmoil of living through a divorce is the number one mental health problem for school-age kids today. Some schools have even started groups for kids of divorce so that they can share their stories and learn from one another how to find their way through the messy business of divorce, building their own lives despite their parents' separation, divorce, or remarriage.

This book is based on a similar idea. We teach a "divorce course" called "Who Gets Me for Christmas?" that kids, parents, counselors, and other teachers helped us design. The book will give you more information about why marriages break up and the legal aspects of divorce, particularly those which apply to you. By better understanding what is happening to you and your family, you can better cope with your feelings about the new situation. Our students have contributed many of their own stories in an effort to help you and others feel less alone and more capable of handling a tough situation.

When parents divorce, kids get hurt—there are no two ways about it. However, through understanding that you are not responsible in any way for the divorce and that hurt and angry adults are apt to behave badly at times, you can begin to adjust to the divorce. More important, you will be able to take steps toward healing and feeling secure and good again about your life.

What's Going to Happen to Me?

1

You'll probably never forget the day you found out your parents were going to separate. Some kids who were only three years old remember every detail as if it happened yesterday. This is an extremely difficult time, and so it's entirely normal to feel all kinds of powerful emotions. The memory of that day will last for a long, long time.

Paula was only three. She remembers her father screaming names at her mother and slamming the door and leaving. Her mother was wearing a red stippled blouse. Paula pushed the door open and ran after her father, crying, "Come back. Don't leave, Daddy."

David was eight years old when his father told him that he was going to live somewhere else for a while, maybe for a long while. It was Halloween, and he'd been excited about going out as an owl, getting lots of candy, and scaring little kids. Now he was scared, and he cried. His mother told him that things would be all right—different but all right. He still cried.

Bruce was nine years old when he found out his parents were getting a divorce. His mother told him the week before he was going to sleep-away camp for the summer that his father would be moving out soon and that they already considered themselves separated. Now, at fifteen, Bruce remembers being "pretty upset" about it. He best remembers begging them to promise that they'd wait until he got back from camp to get the divorce.

Donna got a phone call from her mother announcing the divorce as she sat studying in her dorm during her second year of college. She cried and shook with sobbing all that night. Her roommate tried her best to console Donna, but the hurt seemed too deep and severe to be eased with hugs and kind words.

You may have learned about the divorce in any number of ways. You can be sure it was a terrible day for your parents as well. Parents want desperately to spare their children from pain, but there's no way to make the announcement of a divorce painless. What makes the whole thing unfair is that you didn't do anything to deserve this mess, nor can you do anything to make it go away or even get much better. The lack of control you feel makes the feelings of anger and confusion and pain that are already present much, much worse.

Maybe for a long time, or it could have been a short but intense time, you suspected that something was really wrong at home—overheard conversations, slammed doors, screams of anger, unexplained tear-stained faces. The word "divorce" may, in a way, have been a relief. At least now, with the truth spoken plainly and openly, it removes the subject from the frightening unknown. The limbo land of suspected problems can become a nightmare with looming giants of guilt, rejection, abandonment, and fear. Now the process of grieving over your loss can begin.

Experts who have studied the effects of divorce on children generally agree that *how* the divorce is handled is of the utmost importance to the emotional stability and development of children. If your parents handled the announcement badly, you have an added burden, but one you can manage.

A particularly bad way to get the news is during a screaming emotional scene between your parents. The already frightening news becomes much more horrifying when your parents are hysterical and clearly out of control. "What's going to happen to me?" becomes a most frightening, most real question. If that's the way you found out, you've got to try to remember how much pain your parents were in and forgive them. Rage blows things all out of proportion and causes people to do and say things that are out of character and that they regret later. They probably feel worse than you do about the miserable scene.

If you were singled out and told separately, apart from your brothers and sisters, you may also have some haunting questions. Generally all the children *should* be told together, but often parents choose to handle each child individually. Since confusion and pain set in first, everything appears out of perspective, as if you were looking at everything through a prism or through someone else's glasses. You may ask such irrational questions as, "Why did they tell me first? I must be more responsible for the divorce than the other kids. Why did I hear it last? They probably love me less. They have left me out before, and they probably don't love me anymore, either."

Hold on to the fact that your mind is playing tricks on you. You're searching for reasons in an attempt to gain control. After a while the searching will end, the questions will fade, and real understanding will take their place.

Perhaps the worst way to find out is by surprise. Sometimes parents find themselves so emotionally upset that they never face up to the responsibility of actually telling you.

Sally first found out that her parents were getting a divorce when she came home from a wedding one Saturday to find her father moving the living room furniture into a big truck parked in the driveway. When she went inside, she found his wedding ring on the floor next to a broken wedding picture of her mom and dad. Her father's dramatic scene might have produced the desired shocking effect on his wife, but Sally still recalls the day with tremendous resentment.

There really is no way to make bad news seem good. However, the way you found out about your parents' decision to divorce just had to be a very bad time for you. It's normal to feel miserable.

What should you expect to be told about your parents' decision to divorce? The truth. The decision to divorce is one that will affect all the people involved for the rest of their lives. It's very important that questions be asked and answered clearly and truthfully so that the process of healing can take place. "Don't wait for a year or two years to ask questions," suggests Jeff. "Your parents might want to forget or not want to talk after such a long time. Ask the questions when everything is happening. They are only your parents. They are not going to hurt you or anything."

Some things about the divorce are not your business, nor should you have to hear all the gory details. However, you do deserve to know the reasons why the decision has been made. Often parents feel that in order to protect you, or because you may be too young to understand, half-truths and lies are better. These reasons may be well intended or they may be rationalizations intended to help your parents avoid confronting some hard truths themselves. However, lies make things much harder and more confusing and delay the healing process.

Jeff remembers the early days of his parents' divorce with bitterness. He said, "By the time my mom had given up on asking Dad to come back, I started getting angry at him. I was angry because my mom was telling me all kinds of reasons about why he left. She also told me that he lied to us. For a long time I was angry with him, and I would tell him this over the phone and face-to-face. As time went on, I wasn't angry at him anymore. I know now that everything my mom told me was true, but I accept it now and I forgive him. I feel sorry for him too, because he worries a lot. You can tell from all the wrinkles on his face. He looks ten years older than he really is."

Jeff's story is a familiar one. His father had fallen in love with another woman but wouldn't or couldn't admit it. Rather than say, "I'm leaving your mother for someone else," he chose to give nebulous reasons: "Your mother's a witch" or "I'm just not happy." Then he'd say, "I'll never get married again, not after this," to dispel any idea the kids or the mother had about there being another woman. After a while, a very short while, Marianne appeared and it became clear to everyone that she'd been on the scene the whole time.

Since infidelity is the number one reason for divorce, Jeff's story could easily be similar to yours or those of some of your friends. Although an unfaithful parent may lie about the affair, it's helpful to try to understand the situation from that person's perspective. First, the lawyer undoubtedly has told him not to admit to anything. Second, he probably feels very guilty and overwhelmed with the pain of breaking up the family. Third, he probably has thought ahead and wants you to like the new woman and feels that you might blame her and hate her if you knew he was having an affair with her while he was married to your mother. Also, remember that something had to be lacking in the marriage for your father or mother to find someone else. In time, when things have cooled down, everything will fall into perspective and feelings will not be so intense.

Learning that your parents are getting a divorce is a tremendously hard situation to cope with no matter how you hear about it. You went from day to day expecting things to always be the same: Mom, Dad, you, your brothers and sisters together—a family. When that base of your life becomes shattered, you feel miserable. In fact, you feel so many things so intensely that it's often difficult to get a handle on any of them. It will help you to know that all the things you are feeling are normal. The pain of loss has been broken down and categorized into five phases: denial, anger, bargaining, depression, and finally acceptance.

Maybe an example will help you understand better. Beth wrote, "I was really mad [*anger*] at everyone in my house when the divorce first started. I couldn't believe [*denial*] they were going to ruin my life by separating and Dad not being around. For a while I even tried to get them back together again [*bargaining*]. I didn't think anything would get better for me [*depression*]. It's been about two years now, and I realize that getting the divorce was the best thing to do [*acceptance*] even though I know I'll always be sort of sad for not having my parents together the way things should be in a family."

All these phases are necessary to finally feeling good again. You'll pass through them all in the months right after the separation until you reach acceptance.

Dr. Elisabeth Kubler-Ross first determined these stages in her work with dying patients. In many respects, your parents' divorce is much like a death: You suffer the death of your parents' marriage, and you go through the phases of sorrow. You've lost your family as you knew it and expected it to be—"the way things should be in a family." That's the source of the pain.

It helps to know that the pain is indeed normal, that everyone else who's been through it felt the same way, and most important, that the pain will end.

Dr. Kubler-Ross calls the first stage *denial*. You say to yourself, "Not me. This couldn't really be happening to me." What happens in that first horrible moment when you hear the news is that your mind protects you for a while until you can begin to sort things out and deal with them. This state can be compared to the shock you experience when you suffer a severe physical wound. Often people who get badly hurt don't immediately feel pain. The human mind reacts the same way. We're protected for awhile until we can find a better way to cope with awful news. It's important to get beyond this stage in order to begin healing.

Kristi, who was in the fifth grade when her father decided to leave, said, "I didn't believe him. I thought he was kidding me. Now I realize I probably just didn't want to believe him." Only in looking back after three years could she see that her mind had played a trick on her. She could also see why. She needed the time to find a way to cope with the confusion and hurt of losing her family as she thought it would always be.

John was almost seventeen when his parents announced that they were getting a divorce. For a week he did nothing, said nothing, ate almost nothing, and ignored his friends. It took nearly three weeks before his behavior became anywhere near normal again.

It's a time of hurt, a time of self-pity, a time of not having to think, a time to float along.

If one of your parents is having a particularly hard time dealing with the breakup of the marriage, this stage can be even more difficult for you.

Andrea's mother and father divorced many, many years ago, when she was only three years old. Her mother just couldn't face being divorced and alone. Her religion forbade divorce, and the whole family was embarrassed. So every other day Andrea's mother would hang men's socks on the clothesline for the neighbors to see. Denying that he was really gone prolonged her own torture and certainly confused her young daughter, especially since Andrea had been told that her father was dead. She didn't find out she had a living father until an arrogant elementary school principal confronted her about using an incorrect last name. Her records had shown the truth, even if she didn't know that her parents had been divorced.

Fortunately, in that regard, divorce is more acceptable today, and so tales like Andrea's are infrequent. However, the feelings of intense denial still exist.

One of the healthiest things you can do during the divorce

is to keep out of the center of it and avoid being drawn into the emotional whirlpool your parents may get into. Andrea had to get beyond her mother's problems by understanding the reasons behind them but also by holding fast to the truth. Facing the facts is the beginning of the real process of healing.

The second phase is the *anger* stage. You might ask yourself, "Why me? Why now?" Once it hits you that your parents are separating and that your life is going to be different, you feel very angry. After all, this kind of thing happens to other people, not to you. You feel sad, hurt, and scared, and all those emotions make you darn angry. You feel frustrated because you can't do anything about it, yet it affects your whole life. It's absolutely normal to be furious that such a thing is happening to you.

Bridget lived through years of battles between her alcoholic father and her mother, yet when the divorce started, she was very angry. She said, "My father said to me that on New Year's Eve he'd be moving out because my mother didn't want him at home anymore. I hated my mother for making him leave. I knew why she did it and I understood, but I couldn't forgive her for it."

Matt remembered back over the five years since his parents' divorce: "I was a destructive kid. I threw a book at my best friend in fourth grade. I lived in the principal's office in seventh grade and got into all kinds of trouble in school and on the streets. I cursed at my teachers and never did anything in school or did homework."

Boys tend to act out more. Where girls can cry and talk to their friends, boys take it out in more violent ways. Typical reactions express these feelings. Richie turned into a real monster. "The anger stage I remember clearly. I can recall being ready to challenge almost anyone or anything. Not one morning without a fight, not one night, either. The fights were between me and my friends, me and my parents, me and my teachers, me and my pets, myself and I. I also isolated myself so people who tried to retaliate couldn't hurt me. Mentally, I felt and thought to myself, 'I am indestructible.'"

At least this kind of approach gets feelings out of your system. Another way anger manifests itself can be more damaging. A very tricky and extremely harmful aspect of anger is feeling guilty. Guilt is an attempt on your part to get a hold of the situation, to gain some control over what's happening. Maybe because you acted badly, did poorly in school, and seemed to be the center of arguments between your parents, you are the cause of the trouble and could get things back together. It's similar to the situation of younger children tending to blame themselves for the divorce. Because they are young and still see adults as powerful people and parents as people who "know best," they conclude that they themselves must be problems. However, many child psychologists recognize that self-blame is an attempt to gain control over the situation.

In thinking back over her parents' divorce, thirteen-year-old Kim said, "One of the stages I went through was anger. At first I thought it was all my fault, but then I realized it wasn't. There were other reasons my parents were getting a divorce. It was very hard for me to overcome that anger. It's even still with me today. It's hard to get over, and it's been over nine years."

Anger is normal, but finding a way to express it can be a problem. If you pouted or yelled or stomped around when you were a little kid, you got yelled at or sent to your room.

When you got mad during a sports event, slammed your glove down when you missed a catch, or pushed a kid who had been elbowing or tripping you through half the soccer game, you got accused of poor sportsmanship or were thrown out of the game. Expressing anger usually means getting punished, but experts agree that anger must be let out or it will fester and get worse and possibly make you sick.

Since your parents are already feeling bad, you may also tend to keep all the anger inside yourself to save them any further pain. You may also have figured out they are not capable of doing much for you now, anyway. You shoulder the frustration and confusion and anger in order not to make them feel any worse, but the emotions don't go away by themselves. They also refuse to just lay back quietly in your mind and leave you alone. The feelings will come out somehow and in some crazy forms. Kids who have been through it and have had a lot of stress say that they got into fights, destroyed things during temper tantrums, started hanging around with kids their parents didn't like, and acted terribly in school. Teachers sometimes describe such a changed student as a kid out to self-destruct.

You must find a constructive way to let the anger out in order to begin to heal and feel okay again. Finding ways to let it all hang out can feel uncomfortable and risky. Crying is probably the most obvious release. Just when you thought you'd gotten over crying about everything—grown out of it—you find it a great relief to feel the pain and have it literally flood over you. It helps. So does pounding a pillow or your mattress until you feel exhausted. When Dr. Elisabeth Kubler-Ross visits dying patients' families to help them through the grieving process, she often brings them a length of rubber hose to beat the pillow with so that some of their pain can be released. Keeping physically active can also be a big help. Run a lot, play racquetball, throw a ball against the wall—anything that helps expend the pent-up energy created by your built-up anger.

Another phase of your emotional recovery has been named the *bargaining* stage. When you're confused, you may try to bargain or negotiate your way into some sort of control over the situation. Some people call this "Let's Make a Deal."

Experts have been easily able to recognize the overwhelming desire in young children to bring their parents back together again. Children three and four years old will play with a man doll and a woman doll and put them together in a toy bed or a dollhouse. Six- and seven-year-olds say it clearly, "I wish my mom and dad were together like they're supposed to be." In fact, it's beginning to be clear that no matter how old people are who have divorced parents, they still deeply wish for Mom and Dad to be back together again. Nancy, thirty-eight and divorced, hearing that her mother's second husband had died, immediately thought, "Maybe now she and Dad will get back together." Of course, she knew full well that it was a silly thought, but her heart still leaped at the opportunity for a happy ending.

Perhaps nobody ever really gives up the hope for a "normal" family.

One way you may try to negotiate the two back together again is by playing the "saint." Perhaps because of your excellent behavior and helpful attitude, you can dissuade your parents from splitting. If you've been the center of disputes before, no longer will they have you to fight about. Or maybe you can provide a model of mature, compassionate, understanding behavior to inspire your parents into a new approach toward each other. Katie tried taking on the role of a mother. "I screamed at my younger sister, I yelled at my older brother, and I prepared the meals. I took a lot of Mom's responsibilities on myself, hoping she'd feel better and that Dad would stay." It's a pretty huge task, and usually you just can't keep it up. It doesn't work, anyway.

The more typical role is that of the "devil." The devil hopes that as a result of his rotten behavior and obvious emotional problems, his parents will stay together out of necessity. Danny was really upset about his parents' impending divorce and set his considerable energy toward creating a nightmare for his teachers and, subsequently, the school disciplinarian. A year after life had settled down, he confessed to a favorite teacher that he'd gotten 108 detentions and three suspensions the year before and nothing had worked. His parents had gotten a divorce, anyway. By understanding that the desire to have your parents together is normal, you can better see your schemes as part of the normal process of healing. *Getting on with your life is the important thing. Remember, it's your parents' divorce, not yours.*

Debbie, a very mature teenager, explaining her view of kids trying to mend a broken marriage, said, "It's the love between parents that makes a marriage. If parents don't love each other, kids can't keep them together."

The most painful, sorrowful stage of grieving over the divorce is *depression*. The reality sets in, and you say to yourself, "It's happening." You're in the pits. The familiar life with its promise of security is gone. You may feel such intense pain that you think you'll never get through it.

Another feeling that is similar to depression is *emptiness*. Maria's mother had left home when Maria was only seven, leaving her with her father and an older sister. She said, "I felt a piece of me had left along with her. There was a large space of emptiness inside, a place that could not be refilled even by my mother herself. I felt no one wanted me . . . at the age of seven I thought of suicide. Still I feel emptiness. I don't think anyone in any length of time can help me from feeling that."

The intense pain of emptiness and depression can be so all-consuming that even little things become difficult to do. Friends can't seem to help. You don't feel like talking to anyone. You may spend hours just listening to music and feel totally unable to get up the energy to do the things you used to like to do best.

Hang in there. This too will pass.

Now the good news. You'll finally reach the stage of acceptance and be able to say, "Okay, let's get on with it." You will not feel good about the divorce exactly, but you'll feel more at peace, secure, able to cope with the new situation. Christina, a well-adjusted and happy teenager, said, "Once I accepted my parents' divorce, it was a lot easier to handle. The constant hoping and constant disappointments were no longer a problem. Getting upset happened infrequently and eventually became very rare."

Life will seem good again. Different, yes, but good.

The Loss Inventory that follows was taken from *Perspectives on Loss: A Manual for Educators* by Barbara Bebensee and Jane Rich Pequette. By filling it out, you can assess your losses and better understand why you have the feelings you do and why you behave the way you do some-times. Maybe by facing the fact that you have suffered a substantial loss in your life, you can begin to resolve those feelings and move on.

Loss Inventory for Kids

DIRECTIONS

1. Read the loss listed below.
2. If you have experienced that loss, place an X in the appropriate "time factor" box.

LOSS INVENTORY FOR KIDS	IMPACT FACTOR
Death of parent	10
Death of brother/sister	10
Divorce of parents	10
Extended separation of parents (no divorce)	10
Diagnosed terminal illness—self/parent/sibling	10
Death of close relative	9
Moving to new city	9
Major personal injury or illness (loss of limb, etc.)	9
Abortion	9
Rape	9
Marriage/remarriage of parent	8
Unplanned job loss—self/parent (fired, layed off)	8
Retirement—parent	8
Unwanted pregnancy	8
Changing to new school	8

3. When you have completed the entire inventory of losses, tally each loss as follows: *Multiply impact factor by time factor and enter the answer in the far-right column. Add the total column vertically for your total score.*

4. See score impact information at the end of this inventory.

TIME FACTOR			IMPACT "X" TIME FACTOR
0 – 6 months	6 months– 1 year	1 year– 4 years	
X 5	X 3	— X 1	
	Subtotal		

LOSS INVENTORY FOR KIDS (continued)	IMPACT FACTOR
Major change in a family member (health, behavior)	8
Moved or kicked out of home before age 18	8
Permanent suspension from school	8
Gaining new family member (birth, adoption, relative)	7
Change in financial status of family (much better/worse)	7
Love relationship breakup	7
Death of a friend	7
Diagnosed LD	6
Loss of harmony (conflicts) with parents, teachers, friends	6
Brother/sister leaving home (marriage, college, run-away)	6
Mother beginning work or going back to school	6
Class/teacher/schedule change	5
Sporadic school attendance	5
Moving within city	5
Beginning/end of school	5
Taking new job after school	5
Temporary separations within family (military, business)	4
Change in physical appearance (pimples, glasses, etc.)	4
Violations, of the law (drugs, speeding)	4

TIME FACTOR			IMPACT X TIME FACTOR
0 - 6 months	6 months- 1 year	1 year- 4 years	
X 5	X 3	X 1	
	Subtotal		

LOSS INVENTORY FOR KIDS (continued)	IMPACT FACTOR
Trouble in school (teacher/principal)	4
Change in living conditions (sharing a room, remodelling)	3
Christmas/Easter/vacations	3
Daily success loss (A to B on paper, didn't make team)	3
Argument with friend	3

IMPACT

Under 150: probably have not faced major losses within the last year. It is not that your life is without loss; however, you should have adjusted to the losses that have occurred.

150–300: you are experiencing an average amount of loss in your life. More than likely you have experienced no or very few major losses within the last year. The losses you experienced did cause a change in your life and warranted some adjustment from you. However, there should not have been great confusion and pain with this adjustment.

300–400: may have experienced several high-level losses in the last four years or one major loss in the last year. The losses may have caused a degree of confusion and pain, and re-adjustment may have been difficult and prolonged.

400 and up: probably have experienced multiple high-level losses within the last year. These losses more than likely have affected you physically and emotionally. Adjusting to the losses has been painful and confusing, and there have been major interruptions that you have had to deal with.

TIME FACTOR			IMPACT "X" TIME FACTOR
0 – 6 months	6 months– 1 year	1 year– 4 years	
X 5	X 3	X 1	
	Subtotal this page		
	Subtotal first page		
	Subtotal second page		
	Composite score		

2 Now What?

All the people involved in the divorce—you, your brothers and sisters, and your parents—go through changes. The old life-styles don't fit, and the future may be very frightening. This is a time of uncertainty and flux, and things will eventually settle down. In the meantime, be patient.

Your parents may drastically change the way they treat you. Depending on how well the parent you live with is coping with being a single parent, he or she may become either more strict or more lenient. If a parent is overwhelmed and feels that things are "crazy," he or she may make new rules and regulations that puzzle you.

When things get out of control, people feel insecure, anxious, and nervous. Because of all the adjustments, the newness of just about everything, divorcing parents feel most unsteady and uncertain about life just now. In order to regain their emotional equilibrium, they tend to grab on to something familiar, time-proven solutions that have answered problems in the past. "Hear ye, hear ye. We are now going to have some rules around here," the frustrated, overwhelmed mother may pronounce. "This chaos must end. You kids need rules, and you will obey them." Where dinnertime had been a pretty relaxed affair with everyone sitting around in front of the television, now the family is to sit down together at a properly set table. Saturday morning had been a quick, slapdash sort of cleanup. Now, all dirty dishes are to be removed immediately from the family room upon completion of the snack. Beds are to be made daily and rooms straightened before you go to school.

Studying had always been done whenever you pleased. Now there will be a "quiet hour" between 7 P.M. and 8 P.M. for the purpose of hitting the books. Among the new responsibilities necessary for family survival are doing your own laundry, taking turns doing the dishes, vacuuming the living room twice a week, and mowing the lawn.

Some kids ignore the new rules completely, some resist in varying degrees, and others comply. Remember why these rules have been put into effect: Your parent needs to gain some kind of control over the new family situation. Maybe these new rules will accomplish a sense of security for all of you. At the very least, the house will be neater.

If, however, a parent feels that he or she needs to win your love or feels guilty that you are suffering because of a divorce he or she wanted, you may get away with murder. More than likely, all the new changes will become less extreme with time.

Along with new parenting approaches, your folks may also change their attitude toward you in a more subtle way. Your parents may need you for emotional support. A whole host of new problems come up in trying to manage a household with only one adult to cope with it. Money, bills, broken appliances, baby-sitting, no milk—all the thousand things that may have put your two parents into a tizzy—now fall to one overwhelmed parent. As a teenager, they may turn to you for sympathy. Sometimes you can give them encouragement and help, but be careful to take care of yourself and let them know that you have your own problems.

In discussing problems kids have after divorce, Norma said, "One of the problems that I have in my home is that I am always the psychologist in my family. No one ever asks me if I had a bad day. My family is always worried about their problems, and when they're mad, they take it out on me."

After a while, when things settle down into new patterns, a new closeness may develop between you and your parents based on a better understanding of each other. You've been through a bad time together, pulled together for the good of the family, and grown together through the experience. You've had an opportunity that many people don't have until they're much older: getting to know your parents as people.

One noticeable change may be the way your parents look after a divorce. Being single again after years of being married kind of perks up their interest in being attractive. They may want to look and act younger. Fathers have been known to slim down to fit into designer jeans, buy a gold chain or two, and trade in the four-door Chevy for a sports car. Alice Murray reported on a new group of commuters from the Long Island, New York, suburbs: kids going into New York City on Friday night to see Dad and then returning to Mom back in the suburbs on Sunday. One of the little girls said, "All the fathers look the same. They're all going around with their shirts unbuttoned and gold chains around their necks."

Mothers, too, try to spiff up their appearance. Crash diets (which make for shorter tempers), exercise class, a new haircut, some new clothes—and Mom's a new woman. In talking about the changes in parents, Danny suddenly exclaimed, "Yeah! You know, my mother did lose a lot of weight, got her hair colored, bought a new red car—now she looks like a fox!"

Parents may also act differently from the way they did before the divorce. The changes in behavior are far more upsetting to kids. A feeling of insecurity creeps in when parents behave in an unusual way. The most disturbing of all the changes in behavior has to be seeing your mother or father cry. Here are the persons you have always looked up to, depended on for strength and security—and now they are crying. You feel scared, helpless, and worried. "Boy, this must be pretty bad," you say to yourself. It's an experience that is very difficult for anyone to handle. Larry said, "When I saw my mother and father crying in the living room, I flipped out. I was scared to death. I didn't know what to do or say to anybody, so I ran to my room, slammed the door, and started to cry myself. I was never so frightened in my life." Don't feel it's your responsibility to make them stop crying, but show sympathy when you finally get your own act together. Things will get better.

Sometimes in an effort to avoid the aching loneliness of being alone, parents may run around more, be out all the time. In an attempt to channel some of the energy generated by the pain of the separation or divorce, your parents need to join groups, take up tennis or jogging (as opposed to running around), get out and meet new people, and see single friends. It can be very upsetting for you to have one of your parents living somewhere else and your other parent racing around never home at night.

You feel lonely, too, and need some stability, but right now your parents' needs are so great that their flight is necessary. When Carl's parents were divorcing, he felt very much alone. He said, "My oldest brother and sister are away at college, and my other sister and my mom go out a lot, so I am always alone." Invite friends over, plan your own activities, and be patient. It's a phase. (You've heard that one before, haven't you?)

One obvious change in your family life that you may really resent is an increase in the work you have to do around the house. Not only do the new responsibilities cut into your time, you may interpret them as a punishment for something you had no control over. It's not your divorce, and yet you feel you are paying for it. One divorced kid wrote, "They got the divorce, not me, but I have to pay the price." That's just the way it is. Things have to be done, and now there are fewer people to do them. When it comes right down to it, it won't kill you, and you may even learn a few things about being independent.

These early days of becoming a new kind of family can be puzzling to be sure. It's easier if you can try to understand what your parents may be feeling and, through this understanding, feel more secure and loving toward them. Parents go through a lot of pain during a divorce. Even if one of them has fallen in love with someone else, the pain of leaving the family and familiar life-style can be devastating. The feelings of guilt, anger, rejection, loneliness, sadness, and many, many others batter the spirit and overwhelm the parent going through a divorce.

Guilt. If they'd worked harder at it, been a different kind of spouse, they wouldn't have disappointed their parents and their kids.

Anger. They didn't want this divorce. If only the wife or husband hadn't changed, everything would have been fine. If he or she hadn't left, life would be great.

Rejection. They have failed as a woman or man. They have been found wanting and not acceptable to the person they loved. They failed at the very thing to which they'd devoted their life.

Loneliness. They've lost each other and are no longer part of a couple. Part of their identity is missing. There is no one with whom to share the things of life. Intimacy is gone, an aching memory.

With all this pain so evident, you are probably feeling sympathy and wondering how you can help them. You can't. They have to go through all of it and learn to help themselves. But you can listen to them, understand how they feel, keep yourself together, and be happy doing the things you like to do.

With so many things happening all at once, you may feel overwhelmed and left out. Just as parents are bombarded with powerful feelings, so are kids. Kids' feelings range from being relieved to being confused, sad, lonely, embarrassed, and ashamed. If family life has been filled with friction and fighting, a feeling of relief can immediately accompany the split. "When my father told me," recalls Andy, "I felt very bad but a little bit happy, too, because my parents wouldn't be fighting anymore and it would be calm at home."

Kids can be very confused, especially if they don't understand the reasons for divorce. Morris Schectman of Chicago, who runs seminars on divorce, says outright, "Divorcing people lie ninety-nine percent of the time." That doesn't mean that all divorced people are liars but that the trauma of divorce causes people to behave erratically and atypically. The kids often hear some pretty ghastly things about the other parent and the terms of the divorce. You can get pretty confused listening to all the stories, but in time you'll figure out everything that matters to you.

Feeling sad, lonely, and abandoned is entirely normal when your parents divorce. Although you can intellectually understand that your father or mother left your other parent, you still have been left, and it hurts. Little children fear being abandoned by the remaining parent. Marie, whose mother left her and a sister, felt that no one wanted her. She wrote, "I was sure everyone would leave me. My father proved me wrong, but I felt that way for a long time. When my mother came back two years later and wanted custody of us, my father said, 'There's no way in hell that you will ever take these children away from me.' That's a quote I'll always remember." Abandonment is a natural fear but one that you can handle more easily at an older age. Although you can reject the idea of being abandoned, loneliness can set in very painfully. You miss your absent parent, you miss the old family patterns, you miss a lot. It hurts.

Two of the hardest feelings for teenagers to handle are shame and embarrassment. When the divorce first happens, you may feel that you are the only one who's ever been through it, that everybody else has a "normal" family. You may feel ashamed that your family is different. You may feel embarrassed that your teachers and friends may find out. Somehow you feel that something is wrong with you now. Jennifer put it this way: "I get mad when people say, 'Oh, I'm so sorry your parents are divorced.' It's not *my* divorce." You haven't changed. You are still who you were before the divorce. You have nothing to feel ashamed or embarrassed about.

What can you do to feel better? Basically, there are three excellent plans. One thing many kids find of great help is to talk to a friend, particularly someone who has already been through a divorce. A person like this can really understand what you are feeling and help you anticipate some of the stuff yet to come. You can also get together and laugh over the silliness of many of the divorce war strategies of your parents. Laughter is very therapeutic. Some schools even have divorced kids groups because kids can be so much help to other kids during the bad times.

Finding a friend certainly made an enormous difference for Joe. When Joe flew out to see his father one summer, he had no idea that his mother had decided she couldn't handle him anymore and wanted him to stay in Massachusetts. The day he started school in the east, he didn't even know his address. He was confused, angry, and depressed. He missed his friends back in Phoenix and longed to be back home. Things looked so dismal that he had trouble functioning in school, but then he met Roger in his special reading class. Roger's parents were divorced, too. His mother, in desperation, had fled with her five children, and they all were now living in a motel until the social service agency could find them a permanent place to live. By comparison, Joe's problems seemed less terrible. Roger often came over to Joe's house after school and on weekends. They had a great time together exploring the vast woodlands behind Joe's house. They laughed and giggled over which of the gorgeous girls in the reading class liked them. Joe and Roger became great friends, and this helped both feel better about themselves.

If things are really getting you down and a friend just doesn't fit the bill, you can talk to a sympathetic teacher or a guidance counselor. A friendly ear may be all you need, or you may want to see a therapist on a regular basis to talk through your problems.

Wendy finally could take the pressure no longer. She was deeply ashamed that her parents were divorced. All her friends and, more important, all the kids she wanted to be friends with came from "perfect" families. She tried so hard in school that she got all A's and B's. Wendy auditioned for the school play and belonged to the student council. She did everything right. At home her mother cried and cursed and railed against the unfairness of everything. Wendy tried to comfort and reassure her. When Wendy visited her father, she obeyed all his rules, even the silly ones about leaving anything he bought her at his house.

Then the worst happened. Her mother started seeing a much younger man who didn't want to be bothered with kids. Wendy and her little brother were told that they'd have to go live with their father. Wendy felt betrayed, rejected, and angry and cried all the time. Fortunately, her mother had called the school guidance counselor to tell her of the move. As soon as the counselor asked her about it, Wendy lost control. She cried and sobbed and told her whole story.

The counselor let Wendy come in whenever she felt particularly bad and spent hours with her. Wendy slowly began to feel better and more able to cope with the idea of moving and leaving her mother.

Even with an adult or friend to talk to, you still have to deal with time alone. That can be the worst time. Find new things to do that take a lot of energy and concentration. Dancing, sports, and jogging can expend energy while helping you build a better self-image. Many other activities that require a high level of connection can accomplish the same thing for you nonathletes. Schools are a great place to begin. Usually schools offer a huge variety of "extra" things: dramatics, computer clubs, key clubs, student government, junior achievers. Investigate. It will be worth your while. You forget your problems for a while, and at the same time you really do something for yourself.

With so many changes for both your parents and for you, the relationship you had with your parents just naturally has to change. It's most important that you realize the necessity and establish a new relationship as soon after the divorce as possible.

Usually, one parent will have custody and the other parent, the noncustodial parent, will have visitation rights. Either your parents will decide between themselves how often and for how long the visits are to be or a judge will decide for them. However, you should decide how much time *you* want to spend with each parent. Think the situation through and come to some clear understanding of what you want and need from each parent. It's important to get to know them in new way. If you know what you want, it's a lot easier to deal with some of the tricky situations that may come up later. For example, if each time you go to visit

Dad he has his girlfriend there and you know you need private time with him, ask him for it.

A good place to begin to figure out how all the pieces fit together in a new way is to ask about those things about the divorce which will particularly affect you. Who will have legal custody and when you will visit the other parent are issues you should know about. You also can ask how your basic necessities will be paid for now that one of the income earners is gone. You can also ask who will pay for your educational expenses, including college. These are things you never thought about before, but now they can be nagging questions, even worrisome fears, if they aren't answered. Ask. You have a right to know.

Parents change. You change. Life changes, and you can adjust and learn to grow. Arm yourself with knowledge and understanding, and your struggle toward a normal life once again can be made easier. Somebody said that the only thing that remains constant is change. You've had the chance to experience more than your share, but you will be far ahead of your friends in knowing how to be flexible, accepting, and self-sufficient.

3 The Legal Issues of Divorce for Kids

You may be surprised to see yourself identified as an issue in the legal papers of the divorce. "Issue" is the legal term for a child of the marriage in question. You and your brothers and sisters are discussed in the separation agreement, and important decisions are made by the court about your welfare. You may wonder how some strange man or woman who has never even met you can make decisions about your future, but that's the way it is.

Until you are eighteen, the court has control over what happens to you because you "belong" to the state. That fact is rather amazing in itself. How can that be? The government has recognized that children need a special kind of protection in something called the "Tender Years Doctrine." It's because of this principle that courts can remove children from abusive or neglectful parents. In your case, the court tries to

see that the best situation possible is provided for you and
your brothers and sisters.

In most cases, your parents mutually decide whom you
will live with. In about ninety percent of divorces today,
the children live with the mother and the father is given
visitation rights. However, this was not always the case.

Back in the nineteenth century, when only four to five
percent of marriages ended in divorce, fathers ended up
with custody most of the time. It made sense from an economic standpoint. Since most women did not work, sup-
porting a family was almost impossible. At that time, unlike
today, a father was no longer liable for the support of his
children if custody was given to the mother. To win custody,
the mother had to prove that the father was immoral or had
immoral beliefs.

Things began to change drastically during the twentieth
century. Custody almost automatically went to the mother.
Fathers found themselves fighting the same battles, on nearly
the same terms, as mothers had a few years previously. The
courts assumed that the child was better off with the mother,
and that's all there was to it.

This change occurred because the courts looked very
carefully at what was going on in the family. The father
was going off to work every day, and the mother was staying
home. Laws had been passed to protect young children from
working full time in factories and sweatshops. Mandatory
school attendance laws were being considered in many parts
of the country. Because of all this change, the logical con-
clusion was that kids should go to school, fathers should
go to work, and mothers should stay home to take care of
the children and wait for them to come home from school.

Fathers stopped fighting for custody, feeling that it was a hopeless case.

Thus, the mother got custody, which meant that the kids lived with her and that she was responsible for their well-being. The father got visitation rights, which specified when he could visit his children, and usually had to pay child support. Support money is based on the needs of the child and the father's ability to pay. Either the father agreed to the amount, or the judge decreed an amount he or she thought was fair after consideration of the parents' financial situations.

However, things are constantly changing. Today, fathers are receiving custody more often and judges are beginning to consider options to awarding sole custody automatically to the mother.

Joint Custody

Joint custody is becoming a popular if somewhat controversial alternative to sole custody. The concept is basically that both the mother and the father will continue to share in the parenting of the children after the divorce — an excellent, rational idea. However, the problem lies in defining the specific terms of joint custody. Joint custody can mean either joint *legal* custody, where parents share in major decisions concerning their children's lives, or joint *physical* custody, where both parents share an equitable but not necessarily an equal amount of time with the children. Of course, joint custody can also mean both legal and physical custody.

When Jodi and David's parents got divorced, the children

were only six and nine years old, respectively. It was one of those terrible divorces in which each parent had a tough lawyer, police cars often pulled up in the front of the house when the parents fought, and life was generally hellish. The mother became extremely hostile toward the father and vowed that "he'd never see those kids again." The father was just as adamant in declaring that he wanted to remain an active father and a very present part of their lives. Finally, after considerable time and money had been spent, joint custody was awarded by the judge. Jodi and David were to spend a carefully spelled out *equal* amount of time with each parent. The father agreed to live within a few blocks so that Jodi and David could continue in the same school and have the same group of friends. For three years now they have lived two weeks with the mother and two weeks with the father. On Wednesday they take the school bus to the other house, where they have their own rooms, their own clothes, and all the stuff a kid would have in one home. Everyone involved seems to have adjusted and done well.

The key to joint custody in most cases is that both parents must want it and agree to make it work. Although Jodi and David's mother wasn't happy at first, she learned to adjust and now enjoys her two weeks with the kids and often looks forward to the freedom of the other two weeks alone. If parents agree and can work out the living arrangements, joint custody is a good alternative.

However, divorcing parents often can't agree on anything. What happens then? When your parents can't agree on whom you should live with, it's probably because they see the divorce only as an ending of the marriage, not as an ending to being a parent. The court will then have to decide, based on what is in your best interest, whom you will live with. Usually the court will assign a social worker to the case who will visit with you privately and talk to both your parents individually as well. Based on what the social worker discovers, a recommendation is made to the court. Then the judge may talk to you and ask you some questions. It's sometimes a messy, painful business. You get put right in the middle—between a rock and a hard place—and you may feel guilty and disloyal.

Diane had a terrible time when her parents divorced. She said, "The hardest thing I had to face was making the decision about who I wanted to live with. I loved both my parents very much, and I couldn't pick between them. Naturally I felt something more toward my mom because I was always close to her, but I felt terribly guilty after telling that to the judge. Both my sister and I wanted to live with my mother, but how could we say that in front of our father?

"I think it's unfair to ask a child that in any case. The judge doesn't understand how it is to make a decision like that, especially when that one decision changes your whole life."

If you are put into this situation, there are some things you should remember. First, the judge does not have to abide by what you say. The decision is the judge's to make, and what you have to say is just information to be considered. Usually, if you're thirteen or older, what you have to say carries more weight.

The most important thing to remember, however, is to be clear about what you want and don't want. If you feel strongly that you want to finish high school where you are and your father lives in another town, tell the judge your feelings. If during the separation your parents have been playing games about the visitation schedule, tell the judge that the schedule should be clear and specific. Think things through, write things down, and speak your mind.

When a custody decision is made, it does not mean that the parent who was not granted custody wasn't a good parent or didn't love you enough to fight for you. He or she may just love you enough not to pull you apart in a fight and not to disturb your life anymore.

Unusual Legal Situations

Each case that goes before a judge has its own unique aspects. Because they are all different, it's difficult to discuss specific rulings you may be wondering about. However, perhaps a few of the situations kids have found themselves in may help you understand the workings of courts in dealing with the children of divorce.

When Amy's parents were divorced, it greatly relieved the pressure at home. Her father had been a violent, abusive alcoholic who often beat her mother. Amy lived in constant fear of her father's brutal temper when he was drunk. During some of his drunken rages, he not only hit her mother but also kicked and battered Amy and her little brother.

Her mother's divorce lawyer asked the judge for a court order forbidding the father to see the children in order to protect them. The court agreed.

Many years later, her father petitioned the court to see the children. He'd gone through some rehabilitation programs and seemed to have things under control. The court agreed to let him see the children, but only in a court-supervised setting. A court social worker had to be present during the visit with Amy and Paul. It seemed like a good solution: The father got to see the kids, yet they were protected from possible harm.

Renee's parents finally called it quits after nearly destroying themselves and each other. Their drug use and alcohol abuse had taken a severe toll on them and their two little girls. When the judge heard the gruesome details from these two sad adults, he decided that both parents were unfit and gave custody of the little girls to their grandmother. Sometimes that happens, and it is very tragic.

In both Amy's case and Renee's case, the court was faced with hard decisions. However, they had to be made, and the solutions seemed just.

Mediation

Since divorce has gotten so popular, people have looked for a better way to do it. One idea that has gained much support is divorce mediation. Essentially, mediation is a process in which both parties decide together on a fair and reasonable agreement. The mediator is usually a lawyer or social worker who is specifically trained in bringing together opposing sides in some sort of compromise. It's a way for the divorcing couple to control important aspects of their future. Money and kids rank high on the list of issues to be mediated.

John Haynes, a nationally recognized leader in divorce and family mediation, proposed an interesting concept concerning custody. He suggests that the word "custody" not even be used in divorce agreements. It is a term used only in regard to prisoners and inmates in mental institutions.

He also objected to the use of the term "awarded" as in "awarded custody and visitation." You should not be seen as a prize to be awarded. Also, your father or mother should not be a "visitor" but a parent who has access to his or her children. Rather than custody being "awarded" to one parent and "visitation" rights given to the other, the parenting role that each will play becomes the focus of the decisions to be made.

Mediation sounds sane, doesn't it? If your parents can rise above the anger and pain, mediation can be a great way to work things out fairly.

Since the divorce agreement is between the two parents, their rights are considered and decided upon. One judge, however, felt that the children of divorce should have some rights because they are as deeply affected by divorce as their parents. Yet the children of divorce are not generally represented by a lawyer or spokesperson. The Bill of Rights that judge wrote is not a legal document, and parents who violate it cannot be held accountable in court. However, the concepts embodied in the Bill of Rights are certainly sound, and every divorcing parent would be wise to read them and take them to heart.

Judge Robert W. Hansen of the family court of Milwaukee County, Wisconsin, is the author of the following Bill of Rights of Children in Divorce Actions.

  I. The right to be treated as an interested and affected person and not as a pawn, possession, or chattel of either parent or both parents.

 II. The right to grow to maturity in that home environment which will best guarantee an opportunity for the child to grow to mature and responsible citizenship.

III. The right to the day-by-day love, care, discipline, and protection of the parent having custody of the child.

IV. The right to know the noncustodial parent and to have the benefit of that parent's love and guidance through adequate visitations.

V. The right to a positive and constructive relationship with both parents, with neither parent to be permitted to degrade or downgrade the other in the mind of the child

VI. The right to have moral and ethical values developed by precepts and practices and to have limits set for behavior so that the child early in life may develop self-discipline and self-control.

VII. The right to the most adequate level of economic support that can be provided by the best efforts of both parents.

VIII. The right to the same opportunities for education that the child would have had if the parents had not been divorced.

IX. The right to periodic review of custodial arrangements and child support orders as the circumstances of the parents and the benefit of the child may require.

X. The right to recognition that the children involved in a divorce are always disadvantaged parties and that the law must take affirmative steps to protect their welfare, including where indicated a social investigation to determine, and the appointment of a guardian ad litem to protect, their interests.

This filled-in custodial agreement may help you understand what is considered and help you decide what you'd like *your* parents' agreement to say about you.

Custody Agreement

The custody of the minor child ___Eric___ shall be
                                        (name)
with the ___mother___
            (name person)
Both parents acknowledge their love for ___Eric___
                                          (child's name)
and are aware of the privilege and responsibility of having the child with them. Each parent shall have the opportunity to visit and take ___Eric___ and have ___Eric___ as follows:
                    (child)   (child)

                                      (Holidays) list each

a.   Dad shall have Eric on alternate Christmases

b.   Dad shall have Eric two weekends each month

c.   Dad shall have Eric for spring break plus one month each
     summer

d.   Mom shall have Eric on his birthdays

In order that both parents may have a part in ___Eric's___ upbringing, they agree that _they will share in decisions regarding his well-being such as where he shall attend school and camp, if and when he may get a car, etc._

The husband and wife agree that neither will
___degrade___ the other but will at all times <u>speak respectfully</u>
<u>of the other</u>.

The ___Husband___ shall pay to the ___Wife___ $ 600
per month for the support of the child. This sum shall be
adjusted according to ___the child's needs___ . The
<u>mother and father</u> shall pay for college expenses as follows:
<u>one-half each after scholarships and Eric's own earnings.</u>

Games People Play

The divorce agreement covers the tangible and legal issues, but the more difficult problems are not as clearly solved. Divorce involves a lot of pain, and people in pain often act in hurtful, angry ways. If you have ever had a badly injured pet, you know that you have to approach him cautiously because animals will strike out, bite, or claw in their pain. Anguished adults react similarly.

Parents who are hurt and fighting often have ways of relating to each other that are hurtful to themselves and to you. In trying to negotiate their way through the new and uncertain world of being divorced, your parents may "play games" in order to win control over their lives once again. You may find yourself to be a game piece, a pawn in the games, and you may even play a few of your own.

It's important that you understand a few basic ideas about games:

· They're not fun.
· They're not good for anyone involved.
· They're usually not intentional. They sort of just happen unless you recognize them and avoid them.
· *No one ever wins.*

You really can't preach to your parents about the games they play, but you can learn to recognize the game plan and avoid the whole thing. Through understanding the reasons why your parents get involved with the games and becoming aware of the "rules," you can gain control and put a halt to the debilitating, hurtful games.

On the following pages you will learn the names of some of the most popular games parents play, the reasons for each game, and some possible strategies for avoiding or stopping the game before anyone gets hurt.

I Spy

Did Daddy have his girlfriend over? Was she pretty? Where did Mom get that outfit she was wearing? Did Dad ask anything about me? Who's sleeping in Mommy's bed?

Get the picture? You're asked lots of questions about the other parent as if your purpose in life was to gather information about each parent for the other. The purpose for this game varies. Sometimes your parents simply want to satisfy their curiosity, but more often they want to find out information which will hurt either the other parent or themselves. Often they hope to heal their hurt egos by gathering facts that obviously show that the former partner is not doing well without them. It's a clumsy way of trying to rebuild a parent's damaged self-esteem.

What can you do? You can say, "Please don't try to turn me into a tattletale." You can also suggest that if they want to know something, they should ask the other parent themselves. Only they know best what exactly it is that they want to find out.

Diane, a bright and popular high school freshman, lived with her father but visited her mother each weekend. Her mother had moved out a few years before. One weekend when her mother had asked one too many questions about her father, Diane turned to her and said, "Why should you care?" That comment ended the game quickly. It's difficult not to comply with what your parents want from you, particularly when they are obviously hurt and need support and encouragement. Nevertheless, you're important, too, and should not be afraid to be loyal to your other parent.

Pam put it this way: "I have two lives, the one I'm living with my father and the one I'm living with my mother. They are meant to be separate and not to interfere with each other." Spying on one parent for the satisfaction of the other complicates and confuses your ongoing relationship with each of the two separated parents.

Tug-of-War

It's a tug-of-war, and guess who's in the middle? You feel like you are being pulled from both sides so hard that you'll split right down the middle. The battle rages on, and each side looks for support for "their side." With your approval of their position, their side has more ammunition for the "war" of words and wills. They are then able to assure themselves that they must be "right" and "okay" because you approve of them and can see that the other parent is obviously "wrong."

When Marcia's mother left her father to live with another man, her father was extremely hurt and angry. The whole scene became a nightmarish soap opera of intrigue when the identity of the "other man" became clear. He'd been a family friend for years. Marcia's mother handled things badly, trying to conceal the painful truth. Marcia had been very close to her mother and missed her. After a few months of the father telling stories about her mother's lies and deceitful behavior, Marcia felt that she didn't know her mother anymore and felt that her father was "right."

On the surface, it would appear that this particular tug-of-war had been won. Marcia had been tugged over to her father's side, and he'd become the clear winner. Yeah, Dad! Boo, Mom! Exhausted Marcia.

Actually, however, everyone lost. Obviously, Marcia's mother had lost the respect and companionship of her daughter. However, her father had put a lot of his pain onto Marcia, using her disapproval as proof positive that her mother had been the "bad one" and he'd been blameless and the "good guy." But the real loser was Marcia. The need for a mother is a powerful natural urge. Think of the urgent quest of adopted children who years later seek out the parents who had given them up at birth. Marcia needed her mother and had to see her to resolve the questions and conflicts in her confused young mind.

Messenger Games

Another subtle version of tug-of-war is message carrying.
Warring parents can't stand to talk to each other about anything. Rather than risk the rage of the other parent, they
send little messages with you when you see them. "Tell Dad
he's two weeks behind in his support payment, please,"
Mom will yell as you're running out the door to see Dad.
Can you imagine that line as the opening for a friendly
conversation with your father? Or Dad will say, "Would you
please tell your mother that she'd better get the gutters
cleaned on the house. That place is half mine, and I pay
her plenty of money to keep it in good repair." That would
be a nice greeting for Mom, right?

What can you do if you find yourself caught in the middle? Tell your parents that you love them both and feel very
uncomfortable being caught between them. Ask that they
not involve you in their fights. It's important for you to be
able to love both parents because it makes you feel better
about yourself.

We Still Have Each Other

Sometimes when parents find themselves single again after
so many years as a couple, they become overwhelmed and
feel less than whole. The need for a partner becomes a
gaping hole in their life. They miss the companionship they'd
been sure of, the help and abilities of another adult, and the
strength of someone they'd been able to count on. In an

attempt to fill that need, they may look to you to become the "little mother," the "man of the house," or a "date" for Dad.

At first Ellen was pleased when her father picked her up for her birthday weekend, announcing plans for a "big time" in the city. He bought her flowers, and the two of them got dressed up to go to a play. They stayed overnight in a nice hotel and went shopping together for some great new clothes. Ellen had a good time and loved the new pink cashmere sweater her dad had paid a lot of money for. Months went by after the trip with only an occasional phone call from Dad. He'd started dating the salesgirl from whom they'd bought the cashmere sweater and was too busy to come see Ellen. When his relationship with the salesgirl broke up a year later, he called Ellen and wanted to take her away for a weekend at a nearby resort. Ellen was a year older and wiser and wondered whether she was being amused or used.

The Money Game

The financial burdens of single parents can be crushing to an already overburdened, exhausted parent. When John's mother found herself in an acutely precarious financial crunch one month—two insurance payments were due and the fuel costs to heat the house had skyrocketed—she just couldn't cope with the pressure alone. "John," she said, "I just don't know what to do. We can't make it this month. Both the car and the house insurance are due, and look at this oil bill!" John had no idea what to say or do. He felt insecure and frightened. What did this all mean? Would they have

to move? Could he continue to hope to get a driver's license
next month?

This is a very difficult game to avoid. It can't really be
confronted head on comfortably. You can encourage your
parents to make new friends through their children, particularly after a move to a new neighborhood. Perhaps you
can mention to your parents some places or groups your
friends' parents go. Introduce your parents to your friends'
parents who are in similar circumstances. Above all else,
you can continue to treat your parents as parents, not friends.

Bosom Buddies

When parents find themselves single again, they often feel
like they are starting over and want to be young again. The
old life is gone, and they need to find a way to fit into the
new life, be "with it."

When Joe's parents began a particularly ugly divorce, he
found relief by getting out of the house and practicing and
performing with a rock band. The music was loud, blotting
out the sounds of his parents' battles raging in his mind.
Everyone said he was a terrific singer, and he felt good
about that. One night Joe spotted his father sitting at the
bar where he was performing. "Could that really be Dad?"
he wondered, looking more carefully at the man in the
leather jacket, tight jeans, and—good heavens—that crazy
haircut.

"Hi ya, Joey!" the strange person called. It was he.

Now what?

At first this may not seem like a "game," and it's probably

not as obviously painful as some others. However, it can be confusing and embarrassing to have a parent act like "one of the kids." Tell your parents you need them and are proud of them as parents. Once things settle down and all the family members become more adjusted to their new status, this may even take care of itself.

Anything for You, Kid

Parents generally feel that divorce hurts children. By getting a divorce, they may feel that they've done a terrible thing to you and try to make up for it in some way. Because of the guilt they feel, they may "go without" in order to get you things or buy you very expensive gifts.

In describing his time with his father, Gene said, "I never have to do much when I go over there. I guess in trying to make up for some of the things he did, he's trying to make it up to me. He bought me my own computer to have at his house, and he bought a car for my older brother and sisters."

If you think one parent is more to blame than the other— if, for instance, a parent falls in love with somebody else and leaves to be with that person—that parent feels great pressure to redeem himself or herself in your eyes. However, even the parent who is left feels that you've been hurt and will try to make it up to you.

When Nancy's parents divorced, her mother really fell apart. For a full year Nancy was stuck cooking and cleaning and taking care of her mother. In the intermittent good periods, and finally when things were a little better, her mother showered her with clothes, trips, and lessons of all kinds. Nancy found this phase as uncomfortable as the first. Finally she said, "Mom, you're giving me everything but what I want." What she wanted was her mother's love in a normal relationship. What she told her mother was that her mother didn't need to buy her love.

Over My Dead Body

This is an insidious game that unfortunately is played often. Some lawyers even suggest this game as a way to manipulate the other parent into doing what the client wishes without going to court. It's played to get even with the other parent or to cause the other parent pain by denying him or her the opportunity to see you or have a loving relationship with you. It's "getting even."

When Carl and Jean got a divorce, the battle had just begun. Jean had loved Carl with all her heart, and now she hated him with all her heart. Carl started the game by leaving her for someone else and then breaking into the house while she was teaching Sunday school and taking all his personal possessions. He then stopped paying child support. Jean retaliated by making it next to impossible for Carl to see the two children. She always planned something the kids *had* to do on the weekends Carl was to visit them. She then set out to sign them up for every soccer team, swim club, Girl Scout troop, and gymnastics class she could find so that every weekend would be filled with wonderful things that excluded Dad.

When Carl finally became fed up, he went to court and got specific times to see the children. At 7 P.M. every other Friday he would pick them up, and he would return them at 7 P.M. Sunday. He was to confirm the arrangement by Wednesday evening before his visitation weekend. Okay, now the game had some rules.

Joan saw the judge's ruling as a challenge to her well-developed war games but was undaunted. If Carl had not called by Wednesday, no visit. She'd already made plans. If he was late picking them up, she would have already taken them out. Of course, Carl was no saint, either. He'd bring them back late on the weekends he'd have them or refuse to bring them back to their game, meet, party, or recital. Sometimes he'd say he was coming and not show up. Then Jean would be forced to cancel her plans. The war raged on, with Jean and Carl each scoring points in the endless scrimmages. No one ever won, but the two little girls lost big.

Being older than these two little girls, you can take visitation plans into your own hands. Make certain your parents plan special events and holidays well in advance and encourage them to keep their promises. Let them know how hurt and manipulated you feel when they constantly change plans on each other.

Two versions of this game are much harder to deal with and are beyond your control. The final battle plan could be one parent moving to another state or country so that the visiting parent will no longer be able to see the children frequently. It happens, but not often. Sometimes the courts have stepped in and set a limit on how far the custodial parent may move.

Amanda recently faced this problem. After a long and arduous divorce, her mother and father put the house up for sale and called it quits. Amanda moved with her mother to a large, comfortable house she loved. She was shocked when her mother then announced that she'd gotten a job on the opposite coast. California, here we come. The house sold quickly, and Amanda tried hard to accept the fact she'd be finishing high school somewhere else. Then Dad got mad and went to court to stop his former wife from taking the children that far away. The judge decreed that her mother could not move beyond 150 miles in New York or Connecticut. Now what? The house was sold, her mother had given notice at her current job, and everything she'd just worked so hard to accept was all changed around, with the future looming ahead large and once again uncertain.

The worst rendition of this game, the ultimate in spite and bitterness, is a long drawn-out court battle in which one parent wishes to have the other parent declared unfit as a mother or father. The pain, anger, and money involved in such a final desperate move can debilitate a family for a long time. Nearly all the energy and resources of the parents are poured into the proceedings; once again, no one wins, and everyone except the lawyers loses.

Although these desperate, complex games leave you feeling absolutely bewildered and exhausted, you will survive them. With the courts and lawyers involved, there is little you can do to affect what's happening. You can— must— take care of yourself, however. Your parents are so deeply consumed with strategies and legal stuff that you may feel neglected. Very confusing. Here they are fighting about you, and yet what you feel doesn't really seem to matter.

Stay out of the house as much as you possibly can. Get busy being busy. See your friends, visit an old friend who moved away, or go see your grandparents or a cousin you like. If you can make plans to do things that make you happy, your energy will be redirected in a positive way, one that will make you feel better. After the dust settles from the court scene, you'll have time to deal with the consequences. Worrying about what happens won't help anything, you'll have some great memories to look back on, and those people who you got close to will help you feel better about yourself and could help you deal with what's ahead.

Daddy? You Mean That Bastard?

Or the name could just as easily be Mommy? You Mean That Bitch? This game goes on when the parent who is with the child calls the absent parent names at every opportunity and tries to get the child to do so, too. If it's not name-calling, it's putdowns of one sort or another. However it's played, you find yourself in the middle.

The scene may go like this according to kids who have been there:

MOTHER: Lisa, you better get packed for the weekend because Dad will be here soon. You know I don't want that jerk waiting in the house. What's he got planned, anyway? You baby-sit for his girlfriend's kids, right?

LISA: Mom, why do you put down Dad every time I'm going to visit him? He never says stuff like that about you.

MOTHER: He doesn't talk about me because he doesn't care anything about me, or you either, for that matter. He never would have left us if he'd cared about us.

LISA: Mom, stop it.

MOTHER: He never cared about me or you. He was always on the run. It was either business, golf, tennis, fishing, or women. I can't figure out why you

> want to see him at all. All he cares about is
> himself. That's all he ever cared about.

This particular game has to be dealt with in a straight-forward manner. Because the parent doing the name-calling is so hurt, her (or his) perspective is out of line and one-sided. However, she (or he) absolutely believes she's correct in her perception and may even think you should know the "truth" about the absent parent. Tell your parent that you want and need a good relationship with both of them. Help her to understand that it's difficult for you to feel good about yourself when part of you comes from a "no good" parent. If she doesn't stop, change the subject or leave the room every time the barrage of putdowns begins. Make your own decisions about a parent's character by what you yourself see and experience.

Guided Missile

In this game you become the means by which a hurt and overwhelmed parent, usually the one you are living with, hopes to manipulate the other parent into living the way the injured party sees fit. Divorced parents often have ideas about how a former spouse "deserves" to exist or "should" live. Money often is the central issue.

Maureen's father was really angry when her mother finally gathered the courage to divorce him. He had a very good job and made a more than adequate salary, yet he decided to stop paying child support because he didn't approve of the way his former wife was conducting her life. She'd made many new friends, dated quite frequently, and was enjoying being single. Her new life-style infuriated Dad, and he claimed that he wasn't going to give her money to "run around." Maureen took the situation personally but saw the injustice of the game. She said, "He's not paying child support for me to get back at my mother. He thinks she spends too much money on herself. If I could, I'd tell the judge to get the jerk and make him pay."

Parents also become tempted to play this game if they get jealous when a former spouse finds a new lover. Suddenly Mom or Dad becomes moralistic and protective of your values and refuses to let you visit if the new lover is there. The pain of being "replaced" hurts deeply and can make adults behave irrationally.

Jim had looked forward to spending a weekend with his father, whom he hadn't seen in long time. His father had been busy moving out of the little apartment he'd rented after the divorce and into a cottage on a large estate with his girlfriend, Lorraine. Jim had packed a bag for the weekend before school on Friday, since his father was picking him up as soon as he got home. He jumped off the school bus and raced into the house to encounter his mother looking very grim. "You are not going, Jim," she said solemnly. "I talked to your aunt today, and she told me that Lorraine is living with your father. I won't stand for your being exposed to that kind of irresponsible behavior by your father."

Jim was astounded and had no idea what to say. "But Mom, I want to see Dad," he stammered. "I've met Lorraine, and she's very nice." His mother began to cry and shouted, "No nice woman would live with a man without being married to him."

What could Jim do? What would you do in a similar situation? The truth is that there's nothing much you can do except tell your parents they are making you suffer to get their own way. You might tell them that you don't want to be used as a weapon. Explain that you think that it's pretty unfair and that you plan to do what you think is best for you.

These descriptions and explanations of games are intended to help you if you get caught in any postdivorce melodramas. They are not meant to make parents look spiteful or mean. When people are hurt or under a great deal of stress, they often don't act like themselves. Divorce produces the most stress of any single event that can happen to an adult next to losing a child or spouse through death. The bottom line is that parents can be believed about most things, except each other, during the hard times after divorce.

Games People Play Tally Sheet

For each game listed, check the statement which best tells how many times you've been part of the game.

	Many times	A few times	Only once in a while	Never
I spy				
Tug-of-War				
Messenger Games				
We Still Have Each Other				
The Money Game				
Bosom Buddies				

	Many times	A few times	Only once in a while	Never
Anything for You, Kid				
Over My Dead Body				
Daddy? You Mean That Bastard?				
Guided Missile				

5 The Games Kids Play

In the last chapter we all did a job on the adults. We had fun. Now it's time to reverse the situation and take a look at the games kids play. Kids play games too, but again nobody wins. At first, the divorce may seem an ideal opportunity to use to your advantage, but think it through carefully.

Game 1: "I'll Be on Your Side If You Give Me What I Want."

The aim of this nasty little game is to get something you want by playing up to (into the hands of) one of your parents. When feelings of hurt and anger still haunt your parents, they often delight in hearing bad things about each other—particularly from you.

When Carol's parents were divorced, she felt very bad.

Of her four brothers and sisters, she'd been the one who was closest to her father. Although she loved her mother, they were not very close and didn't see eye to eye on much of anything. Her father lived across town with his girlfriend, who soon after the divorce became his wife. Carol visited them each Sunday until she went to college fifty miles from home. She'd gotten a scholarship and lived on campus but enjoyed bringing friends home for weekends. One particular spring weekend Carol called home to tell her mother she'd be coming home with a friend. Her mother had plans for the weekend and said, "Look, Carol, instead of calling to *tell* me you were bringing a friend home, why don't you *ask* instead?"

Carol was furious. She'd show her mother. She'd call her father and stay there. She hung up the phone with a crash and dialed her father's number. "Dad, you know what a pain Mom is," she began, and from there she was pretty sure she'd get exactly what she wanted. Not only were Carol and friend greeted with open arms, they got the royal treatment all weekend long. Her father and stepmother delighted in being more open and understanding than Carol's mother had been. Dad felt more justified in leaving his first wife. After all, even her own daughter could see she was a pain.

Did Carol win? It sure looks that way. She got what she wanted and more. But at what cost did the victory come? She had been disloyal and insulting to her mother just to get her own way—a pretty high price for one weekend of fun. What might happen to Carol when Dad decides that his weekend plans are more important than hers? What can Carol do to get back in the good graces of her mother? Was her mother unreasonable in her request?

Game 2: "But Mom Said Yes."

The goal in this game is similar to the goal in game 1: to get your own way at the expense of one of your parents. It can also provide you with a way of punishing one parent for something real or imagined that he or she did to you.

Dina's parents' divorce had been a pretty mutual decision, and her parents had remained somewhat friendly until her father found a much younger woman and moved in with her. Dina's mother had gone back to work full time and was really struggling to do well at her new job; deal with Dina's older brother, who'd gotten heavily into drugs; take care of her other two children; and find a new circle of friends for herself. Life at home was chaotic, and many of the everyday household chores fell to Dina. By comparison, her father's new life was a dream. His young girlfriend was pretty, energetic, and exciting. Dina liked her a lot and thought her father was "really cool." Mom, on the other hand, was a drag. All she ever did was nag and complain, and she had made up all kinds of new rules to keep the home somewhat together.

Dina came home from school one day all excited about going to a rock concert. One of her brother's friends had somehow managed to get the expensive, hard to find tickets for the concert in a neighboring state. She figured that her mother would say no, so she'd need a plan in order to be able to go. Step one: Clean the house. A nice touch. Her mother would be grateful and see how mature she was.

As she busily vacuumed up the crumbs of stale potato chips from the rug in front of the television set, she got a great idea: Call Dad first. He'd be sure to say yes. He was really cool, and Ingrid, his girlfriend, had told her just last week how much she loved the group Dina planned to see. Brilliant!

Dina threw down the vacuum cleaner and called her father's office. Sure enough, he thought it was wonderful that she'd gotten tickets. Why not! Yeah, all right! Super. She was as good as on her way.

When her mother got home, Dina told her all about her plans. Her mother hit the roof. No way! It was crazy to pay all that money to see a concert. She was too young to go that far *that late*. Her brother's friend who'd gotten the tickets was not to be trusted. He'd already totaled one car that the mother knew about. Forget it!

Dina smiled inwardly. When to play the ace? When her mother was exhausted from the argument, Dina dropped it on her: "But Dad said yes."

Bingo! The confusion and defeat flashed across her mother's face. Dina knew that her mother was jealous of her feelings for her father. Her mother resented being put in the role of disciplinarian all the time while Dad could be the good guy. Dina had carefully and quite skillfully backed her mother into a corner.

What could her mother do? Either way she would lose. If she said yes, she'd feel weak and manipulated. Dina might have won a skirmish in her battle for independence and doing what she wanted, but at the price of being dishonest and unfair, neither of which is a good thing to be.

Game 3: "If You Remarry, I Won't Visit You."

This game could be called blackmail. You use the power you have to try to prevent your parent's new relationship. You know that your visits to your parent mean a great deal and threaten to stop going if the new, objectionable relationship continues, particularly if the parent begins talking about marriage. You may initiate this game because you fear losing the present relationship you share with your parent or because you just don't like the new person and hate being around when he or she is there.

Katie's parents' divorce was a classic: Her father ran off with Sally, his secretary. Katie hated Sally. Not only did Katie blame Sally for the divorce, she couldn't stand Sally as a person. Katie made life pretty miserable for Sally during the weekend visits with her father, who shared an apartment with Sally. Each time Sally would ask her to do anything, Katie would oblige but always with a shrug or a slight grimace, a whine, or some little thing designed to be irritating but defendable if Dad got in on the act. Sally was young and felt insecure with Katie and her sister and finally quit trying to be nice to the two resentful girls. Things got worse, and Sally was labeled "mean," "stupid," and "a jerk" by the girls. Katie told her father over and over, "If you marry her, I'm not coming here again."

One week after the divorce became final, Katie's father married Sally. Katie grudgingly went to the wedding "just to get the new clothes" her father had bought for the occasion. Did Katie lose this game? You bet. She lost *big*. Not only did her father marry Sally despite her threats, but Katie became a blackmailer along the way. Most important, she damaged her relationship with her father and his wife. Kids can't break up a relationship if it's a rewarding and fulfilling one for the parent. They aren't powerful enough, nor should they be. When faced with a situation like this, you should try to understand that your parents have been through a really hard time, just like you, and now they are working on being happy again. If they are happy, you'll have a much better chance at being happy, too.

Game 4: "Watch Out For Me, I'll Get Even With You Somehow."

The last and most harmful game is called, "Watch Out for Me, I'll Get Even with You Somehow." Unlike the previous games, in which the kid involved calculated the goals and strategies, in this situation the kid rarely understands either the motivation or the consequences. Subconsciously the kid involved is displaying deep hurt and anger by acting quite differently from the way he or she acted before. The new behavior can range from a passive retreat to a more violent acting out against others or himself.

Kurt's behavior clearly illustrates this pattern. He said, "Right after my parents' divorce (the second divorce for me to go through), I went to school just for something to do during the day. Well, my grades went down, and you couldn't say much for my behavior. I got in so much trouble, it seemed like the only part of the school I saw each day was the inside of the principal's office.

"One day I got in a fight in school, and both my parents

were called in for a conference. I was really embarrassed because my parents got in a fight about whose fault it was that my behavior was so bad. The principal almost got punched out by my father for interfering in family matters.

"After that day I was embarrassed and afraid to go into school for fear that I would be teased by my classmates. But after a while I got over the whole incident and my grades came back up. The divorce of my parents was not the end of the world, and now I realize that."

Tracey had a harder time after her parents' divorce. When her parents split up, she chose to stay with her father. Her parents had agreed on a joint custody situation in which she would live one year with each parent. When the first year was up, Tracey moved 250 miles north to live with her mother, sister, and new stepfather. She really missed her friends and felt victimized by the move. She'd hated her father's girlfriend and two kids, who'd moved in right after her mother had moved out, and she felt as if she'd been "kicked out."

In September she started a new school. Tracey was extremely intelligent and very friendly and had exquisite manners. Things went pretty well until Christmastime. She'd looked forward to going "home" to her father's and seeing all her old friends. She even thought she'd like to see the "brats" again: the girlfriend's kids. Shortly before the Christmas vacation began, her father called. He felt it "would be better" if she stayed with her mother for the holidays. He and his girlfriend had just gotten married, and he wanted to get used to his new family. Disaster, despair, depression. Tracey felt rejected and was so severely hurt that she felt pushed toward some kind of demonstration of the pain. She wrote a note about suicide and left it where her mother could find it. Her mother became deeply alarmed and alerted her teachers and guidance counselor.

Her father thought she was just being dramatic. His seemingly callous dismissal of her desperate thoughts angered and hurt her more. For the rest of the year, Tracey went rapidly downhill. Although an A-plus student, she received four F's on her next report card. She stopped doing any schoolwork at all. Rather than go out with friends, she spent hours in her room reading. She read voraciously, skipping lunch at school to read. She lost all her friends and began to look disheveled. If she didn't actually take her own life, she gave up some wonderful parts of it in a desperate attempt to express her pain.

Tracey needed professional help at this point in her life to help her cope. Fortunately, her parents sought out a fine psychiatrist who helped her pull out of her destructive behavior pattern. Other kids aren't so lucky.

In the beginning of the divorce, you may actually win one or two of these games. This could be the way to get something out of this mess for yourself and feel some kind of control over the situation. However, in the long run you'll end up feeling guilty, untrustworthy, and depressed about playing these games. The best way to control the situation is for you to be up front and direct with your parents. By trying to understand why they are acting the way they are, you can then determine how you might change the situation.

To help you avoid games and adopt a positive approach to your problems, you might try using the outline that follows. It guides you through a logical strategy for considering tough problems.

If something is really bothering you, you must first think

through the problem carefully. After analyzing exactly what the problem is, you can then go on to explore different solutions before deciding on a course of action. Before you do anything, think through the possible reactions your parents may have. Be sure to figure out what the worst and best responses might be before you are stuck with the consequences of an ill-thought-out move on your part.

Following the outline, there is a case study and a filled-in version that demonstrates how to use it.

Problem Solving

I. *ANALYZE*—To fully understand a problem, you must try to see both sides of the issue as clearly as possible.

Your side _____

_____

_____

Parent's side _____

_____

_____

II. *COMPROMISE*—Since a person can be responsible only for his or her own behavior, the next step is to determine what the person can do to change the situation.

You can _____

_____

_____

You can ask that _____

_____

_____

You can reasonably expect the parent's response to
be _____
_____
_____

III. *THE BOTTOM LINE*—After clearly thinking through a
problem and exploring solutions, a person must decide
on a course of action (or inaction) and be willing to
accept the responsibility for it and the reactions to it.

The bottom line is that you _____
_____
_____

IV. *RESULTS*—It's best to think through the possible reactions in order to be prepared for them.

The best you can expect is _____
_____
_____

The worst you can expect is _____
_____
_____

CASE STUDY

Jayne lives with her father and older brother. Her oldest
brother is out of state in college. Her mother moved to a
nearby town six months ago, when divorce became immi-
nent. Jayne can't figure out what's happened to her mother.
First she left home, and now she seems to be lying to her
a lot of the time. Mom spends all her time with her new
boyfriend and sometimes doesn't show up or comes very
late when they have plans together. Jayne feels confused,
rejected, and angry. What can she do?

Problem Solving

I. *ANALYZE*—To fully understand a problem, you must try to see both sides of the issue as clearly as possible.

Your side   I feel like Mom's rejecting me and treating me unfairly. She lies, and that makes me feel very hurt.

Parent's side   Mom's trying to find a new life. Her boyfriend is very important to her. She sees her responsibility to be to herself now.

II. *COMPROMISE*—Since a person can be responsible only for his or her own behavior, the next step is to determine what the person can do to change the situation.

You can   tell her I'm happy she's finding a new life that she's happy with and am pleased she's found a man to love. Tell her I feel hurt by her actions, however.

You can ask that   she tell you the truth. She can be on time if she makes plans with me.

You can reasonably expect the parent's response to be   to listen and try to understand. Stop lying and come on time.

III. *THE BOTTOM LINE*—After clearly thinking through a problem and exploring solutions, a person must decide on a course of action (or inaction) and be willing to accept the responsibility for it and the reactions to it.

The bottom line is that you   will leave after waiting for Mom for fifteen minutes

IV. *RESULTS*—It's best to think through the possible reactions in order to be prepared for them.

The best you can expect is <u>Mom will understand and follow through on time with scheduled visits.</u>

The worst you can expect is <u>Mom won't bother to see me at all.</u>

At least you know where you stand.

6 Living with Single Parents

The period right after a divorce is a very bad time. It seems that everything that once was predictable and secure is now uncertain, and the future seems a bit frightening. Kids generally agree that it usually takes eighteen months to two years for things to settle down and feel "normal" again. Those months are difficult for everyone. In the confusion of finding ways to cope with the changes in your life, your feelings may be exaggerated and out of perspective. A normal yet totally unrealistic feeling that creeps to the surface is guilt. You may feel a sense of guilt about your role in causing the divorce. When a lot of things are left unanswered, you seek answers within yourself.

Feeling Guilty

Bob, whose parents divorced when he was eleven, said, "I felt like my mom and dad were getting divorced because of me. They told me my mom might be leaving for a little while during the summer. The next thing I knew, my mom had gotten an apartment in another town. I thought I'd done something really bad that made my parents fight. I felt my parents didn't love each other or me.

"They told me it wasn't my fault, which was a big relief to me. I felt really bad for my parents, my sister, and me."

Bob was thirteen when he wrote that and obviously remembered those awful moments vividly. He now lives happily with his father, and his sister lives with their mother. Bob sees his mother often and likes her boyfriend.

Sometimes the guilty feelings continue beyond the initial adjustment period. When guilt continues, the feelings are more pervasive and gnaw at your sense of self.

Gina talked about her feelings clearly when she said, "One thing that bothers me the most about my parents' divorce is that no matter how hard I try to tell myself that I don't have to choose which parent I love more, I always feel that I have to. I am afraid that because I choose to stay with my mom, my dad will feel upset. I am not very close to my dad as it is. I cannot get myself to realize that I did not get 'divorced.' It seems that everywhere I go and everything I do, I have to think, 'Is this going to hurt Dad's feelings?'

"I feel because I live with my mom, I don't love my dad. When I think about the possibility of going back to live with Dad, I get sick. I was not happy there at all. I have a great life now, and living there would be the pits. I still feel I'm cheating my father out of something. I try hard not to think of it like that, but it sure seems that way."

No matter how powerful the feeling of guilt may become, you must remember—keep right up front in your mind— that a marriage or a divorce happens between adults. Diane said it best when she remarked, "Parents break up a relationship or put it back together again."

Money Problems

Guilt is a ghost, but fear is real. You probably will experience many feelings of fear about things both real and imagined. So much has happened that many of the things you'd always taken for granted now appear problematic. Money, a central issue in any divorce, has far more importance to the single-parent family than it ever had before. During the whole separation process you probably heard the word "money" a million times. Mom was afraid she wouldn't have enough, Dad thought she wanted too much, and so on and so on. The idea of not having enough money can be very frightening. Being "poor" is an awful thought.

Anthony stated, "I hate when my father doesn't give my mother the check on time and somehow she always blames me because I'm closest to my father and I'm almost always with him. Finally, I had to tell her to stop yelling at me about the money, that I had nothing to do with it. Tell him. Yell at him, not me." Finally she did.

In ninety percent of divorce cases involving the custody of children, the kids live with their mother. National statistics show that women still earn about 60 cents for every dollar a man earns. With Dad gone, usually taking the majority of the family income with him, the mother and children lose a substantial portion of money. Law professor David Chambers spelled out the financial problems of divorced families in *People* magazine. He said, "A woman with a couple of children typically needs about eighty percent of the family's former income to continue at the same standard of living. A typical court order would provide roughly thirty percent of the father's take-home pay if he'd been the sole wage earner before." With only thirty percent of the family income, which often is irregular or nonexistent, a single-parent family certainly has some huge adjustments to make in its life-style.

How can the family members make it? Somehow they do. Very few kids complain about the lack of money, so it seems that mothers somehow manage to make ends meet. You should be aware of the new financial situation but not be consumed by it. One thing you can do is investigate ways to be financially independent to some extent. If you're under sixteen, you'll probably have to be quite creative to find a job, but you can find a way.

Because of the fact that one parent no longer lives with you and maybe pays "support," you may feel a bit unsure of what, if anything, you can ask of your parents in the way of money. Many noncustodial parents also are very sensitive about being "used" only for money if kids ask for too much too often. However, this person is still your father or mother, and you should feel able to ask for those things you really need or are too expensive for one parent to fund individually.

Perhaps the hardest thing to handle can be parents who are so intent on the divorce wars that they behave in an immature way that hurts you. Money is a very tangible issue and therefore ripe for war games.

Allison's parents couldn't call an end to the war even after the divorce was final. Allison was always caught in the middle, feeling tugged at and strangled by the money issues between her parents. Allison said, "The biggest problem I've been faced with since the divorce pertains to money. This past year, I've gone to many of my friends' birthday parties, and I usually brought a gift that cost about ten dollars. When the first party was held, it was my mother's responsibility to get a gift. My father wouldn't give me any money. I went to more and more parties, and my mom kept paying. Then, once she refused to pay for one, so I asked my dad, who was a little stubborn about it, but he gave me the money.

"Last year I had dancing lessons, which I'd wanted to take for a long time, and Mother provided all the money and transportation. This autumn and past winter I had dance lessons again, and my father paid this time, and Mom and Dad shared the transportation. This coming Monday the lessons begin again. My mother complains she cannot pay, and my father says he will pay only half. 'It's a matter of principle,' he always says. He will only pay half, and mom won't pay at all. I offered to pay half myself, but neither would allow that. If neither of them pays, I won't be able to go, and these lessons mean a great deal to me."

Each year, the eighth grade class in Todd's school got to go on a trip to Washington, D.C. The whole week cost $140. Todd knew immediately he'd have trouble asking for that much money from his mother, who worked extraordinarily hard to make ends meet. He came up with a plan. He'd work hard in the school fund raiser selling light bulbs and ask his parents to split the balance. He worked so hard that they only had to pay $25 each, and they readily agreed to Todd's fair and reasonable request.

Sometimes when parents divorce, kids have to move. Either the judge orders the house to be sold so that each parent gets a share of what the house is worth or the expenses on the house are too great for the mother to handle.

Karen's parents got a divorce when she was in the fifth grade. The house that the family had lived in cost a lot of money to maintain, and so Karen, her older brother, and her mother moved to a little rented house. Karen changed schools. At the end of the seventh grade, her second year in junior high, she moved again. The landlord had decided to sell the house, and her mother couldn't afford to buy it. The new apartment was very close to her new school, and Karen grew to like walking to school; her older brother, who was in high school, loved going home for lunch. When Karen was a sophomore, her mother decided to marry the man she'd been going out with and move to his house in a nearby state. Karen moved again. Since friends are so important to teenagers, each move meant good friends left behind and anxiety about being new, fitting in, and finding new friends. Karen rose to each occasion and learned to make new friends while staying in close contact with the friends she'd left behind.

If you find yourself in a similar situation, you'll probably feel as resentful and fearful as Karen was. A move normally causes real feelings of loss. You go through all the phases of sorrow that you did when you heard about the divorce. But you can be sure that you'll adjust to the move, too.

Making plans to visit old friends and have them visit you can really help in the transition. Somehow you know you'll make new friends who will add new and exciting dimensions to your life.

Perhaps the biggest fear for older teenagers of divorced parents can be money for college. When parents live together, you can be pretty sure that somehow you'll be able to go to college. From your earliest birthdays you may remember getting money that your parents banked for you for college. Now what? Will there be money? How can Mom help out when she already is stretching every dime? Will Dad pay anything?

Sometimes the separation agreement includes a provision for college expenses. If you don't know whether your college expenses have been arranged for, ask. If college was not included in the agreement, that doesn't necessarily mean that your parents will not pay your college costs. It simply means that this was not included as part of the separation agreement. To find out what you can expect, ask your parents what they plan to do to help with college expenses. You may be very relieved to learn that they have thought it through and have every intention of seeing you go to college.

If, however, you sense that you are going to have difficulty with money, it's best to know now so that you can plan ahead. Don't despair. You should see your high school guidance counselor and explain the situation. There are countless sources of aid for deserving kids who want to go to college. There are special programs for kids whose family income falls below a certain figure. In fact, many people who are not divorced joke that perhaps they should get a divorce so that their kids will have a chance for scholarship money. Some joke, but the truth behind the story is that money is there for kids like you. Find it. Go for it.

Having to Do More Because There's Less

Sometimes the crush of financial problems falls squarely and quite unfairly on your shoulders. When Megan's parents divorced, her father left the family in a real financial mess. Megan's mother hadn't worked in years and had to renew her training as a nurse; she then got stuck taking the only shift the local hospital had open, the late shift. If she paid a baby-sitter while she worked, her meager salary would not cover the family's expenses. She therefore decided that Megan was old enough to take care of baby Courtney.

From the time Megan was eleven, for three days each week she had to pick up Courtney at a neighbor's house, walk her home, watch her all afternoon, fix supper for them both, give her a bath, and get her ready for bed. Her mother arrived home at 8:50 P.M., just in time to tuck Courtney into bed. For five years Megan baby-sat for Courtney while her friends were free to join after-school clubs and hang out together in town. It wasn't until Megan turned sixteen that she finally was relieved of the responsibility of her sister's care and allowed to get a paying job of her own.

Debbie found herself in a similar situation. She began baby-sitting for her little sister when she was in seventh grade and her sister was in first grade. She had the responsibility for Donna not only after school but also on weekends when her mother went out. Donna was a difficult kid with a mind of her own. She resented taking orders from Debbie and taunted her constantly by threatening to "tell." "I'll tell

Mom you spent two hours on the phone if you don't let me go over to Suzie's house." Their forced time together proved to be a battle of wits—power plays to determine who had more dirt on the other.

In thinking about those days, Debbie wrote, "For one thing, I've decided I'm never going to have kids." She also noted a vast difference between baby-sitting for neighbors for money and having to take care of a brother or sister. She said, "When you watch a brother or sister, you have more of a tendency to be after revenge, like, 'You told Mommy I had Sally over, now you have to go to bed early!'

"When you aren't making money for watching the kid, you get so mad inside that you have to stay home when everyone else is going out and having fun that you storm around the house, slam doors, and everything else. Watching kids when you really don't want to is tough not just on you but on the child. You react in unwise ways to everything the child does wrong."

Both Megan and Debbie resented, to different degrees, the load of responsibilities that had been dumped on them. "For heaven's sake," remarked Megan. "Some kids I knew were having baby-sitters themselves, and here I was spending my life being a baby-sitter." Megan pulled through in pretty good shape. She worked hard in school and had high aspirations for an independent life for herself after high school. Debbie, however, rebelled at the situation she found herself in during high school. Although her mother depended on her for so much, she failed to give her the attention, approval, and recognition Debbie desperately needed. Debbie performed adult tasks and took adult responsibilities while she was still a little girl herself. She was robbed of a childhood and entered her late teens without the foundation of good feelings about herself necessary for her to be successful and happy. After months of screaming fights with her mother, truancy problems at school, and days at a time away from home, Debbie's mother brought her to court for being incorrigible. Debbie spent two years in a residential state school, where she graduated with an impressive academic record after having served as an officer in the student government.

Her natural intelligence and strength of character shone through the problems of her life. Today she has an apartment of her own, holds down two part-time jobs, and goes to college nights.

Debbie's younger sister, Donna, is now thirteen and looks back over the years she was in Debbie's charge with mixed feelings. "I hated taking orders from her. Your mother is *supposed* to tell you what to do, not your sister. I got mad at her a lot, and I guess I was a real pain sometimes.

"I think it made us closer, though. When Mom and Debbie would have a fight, I always would take Debbie's side."

What can you do if you find yourself overloaded with responsibilities? First, you've got to try to see the whole picture. Your parent probably would not expect you to do so much if it didn't seem necessary. However, that is not the whole picture. You have things to do and friends to be with that are also necessary. Being a kid is a big part of becoming an adult. Because your mother is struggling so hard to make a new life for all of you, you may go on being miserable and feeling cheated and then feel even worse— guilty—because you resent what you have to do. Somehow you must get up the courage to explain how you are feeling to your mother. Easier said than done. It takes real courage. You may need help. Talk to your guidance counselor, a

trusted teacher, or an older friend. They can make sugges-
tions on how to approach the subject and give you moral
support. Getting your feelings out in the open with your
mother may be difficult—it may even make things worse
temporarily—but once things are out in the open, solutions
are at least possible. You'll feel better in the end.

Feeling Different

What about the other things—less tangible things than money
and not having enough of it—that cause pain and fear?

Although the statistics indicate that between forty-five
and fifty percent of marriages end in divorce, you may still
feel different and be embarrassed that you're an outsider in
the American dream of a mother and father, a boy and a
girl, and a station wagon. A million kids a year join the
ranks of "divorced" kids, yet most kids feel isolated, as if
they were the only ones with problems like theirs.

Beth feels very angry at being different. Her mother
immigrated to this country and was overwhelmed when her
marriage broke up. She felt lost and scared and tried desperately to shelter and protect her two daughters. "I feel
like an oddball," Beth said. "Other kids tell me about their
families and what they do. What can I say? My family is
divorced, and we don't do those family things. When people
bring up family things, I just don't say anything. It's hard
to deal with, and it's been nine years."

Some psychologists say that there are two types of families: the "open" and the "closed." Beth's family epitomized
the closed type of family; they had few friends outside the

immediate family. The role of the woman and the role of the man were narrowly and clearly defined. Children had their "place." Exposure to the outside world was limited and restricted to church groups and people of their own ethnic origins.

If your family seems to be similar to the closed type, you may have a more difficult time adjusting to the divorce and feel more deeply hurt. Your resources for support may be more limited, so you'll have to actively seek out help. A favorite trusted teacher or your school guidance counselor may be a good place to begin. Having someone else know about your feelings who is outside the closed little world your family has existed in will be a beginning toward feeling better. Such a person can help you understand and feel comfortable in a friendly world where people care for you. The more potential for yourself you can begin to see and experience, the quicker you'll begin to feel better.

The open family is quite the opposite. The main characteristics of this family type are openness and activity. They have many friends and have done many interesting things both separately and as a group. They are more likely to have talked about the divorce before it happened and are less afraid to reach out for help and guidance. It would seem that this group would have a far easier time adjusting to a divorce. However, sometimes these worldly, well-put-together types can display a false bravado and rationalize away the pain and anger or refuse to recognize it at all.

The First Year Is the Hardest

In many ways you may feel different at first, but soon your life will become familiar—normal. As you gain a surer sense of yourself, you'll feel okay and not odd. Your life will continue regardless of what has happened to your parents.

During that difficult first year, your life seems so bound up with conflict, chaos, and changes that it's hard to keep a healthy distance and avoid becoming bogged down by the divorce. Your parents have so many new problems that they may not be able to do much to help you at all for a while. In fact, they may add to your problems when they have difficulties coping and take their frustrations out on you. A typical comment about living through this difficult time of adjustment is, "If my mother would calm down a little and stop being pushed around so much, she wouldn't be so grumpy." Another frequent complaint is, "I get mad when my mother yells at me when I did nothing wrong."

Sometimes a parent can make life even more difficult. Johanna's mother often put her daughter in a very uncomfortable position when she was "too busy" to drive the endless car pools that go with suburban living. Johanna said, "The thing that bothers me most about my parents' divorce is that they make me depend on other people too much. My mom will say, 'Oh, Michele's mother will understand that I can't pick you up. She'll drive you home.' My mom hates it when something like that happens to her, so she should understand it's not fair. I feel guilty at expecting my mother to drive when it interferes with her life, but I don't like putting other people in a bad position, either."

Parents can certainly seem selfish, and for a time they just might be. It's tough to go through a divorce. If things get too hard to handle, talk to someone about it. Friends can help by listening. There are also adults out there who will listen and help.

If you are lucky enough to have grandparents who live nearby or whom you talk to or see often, they can be a tremendous source of support. They love you very much and also love your parent. They're probably feeling very bad for all of you and don't know how to help. They may fear "interfering" but want to do something for you or for their child who is hurting. By talking with them, you may not only feel better yourself, you may help them talk out some of the pain.

When asked what advice she would give to a kid going through a divorce, Paula, a veteran of two divorces, said, "You've got to see your parent as an honest person. If you see your parent as dishonest and deceitful, that is how they are going to see you." Gerald agreed readily and went on: "You've got to establish the relationship with your parent early. Ask them right away about the divorce. If you wait until later, they sort of want to forget it. They're your parents, after all. They aren't going to hurt you or anything."

The Long Term

A new and different life-style finally begins to develop after the initial adjustment period. You have settled into a regular pattern that now seems normal. You may have moved and made new friends. Your parents seem to have gotten a much better grip on the situation. For the most part life is calmer, quieter, and more peaceful at home.

Not only does life feel normal, good things can also happen. The best part about living with a single parent is the good relationship that develops between you and that parent. Usually, when life settles down for your mother, she can relax and begin to get to know you on a new level. You have more to say about things and are included in many of the decisions. The first thing kids mention when asked for the positive side of divorce is that they have become much closer to the custodial parent. Just as the pain of divorce brings out the worst in people, the healing process often brings out a person's strengths. You've known your parent through it all and can better appreciate the parent as a person and respect him or her for who he or she is rather than just because that person is your mother or father. Some people never become friends with their parents.

So Your Parent Dates

Although your relationship with the parent you live with gains new depth and meaning, it's important for both of you to realize that adults need adult relationships. With Dad or Mom gone, no matter how bad the relationship was, a huge vacuum is left in your parent's life. Holidays, vacations, and visitation days can be very lonely for a single parent. One solution to the loneliness problem is dating.

Since most of their friends are married, they don't fit anymore into the social life they'd had. Finding a new social life can be a really frightening experience. Are they attractive enough to be appealing to the opposite sex? Where can they meet an available man or woman?

Somehow most parents usually connect, and this may create new anxiety for you. You wonder how all this is going to affect you.

Eric found himself feeling abandoned when his mother started dating seriously. His older brothers had left for college that fall, and the quiet in the big old house made him afraid. He'd looked forward to being the "only child," but somehow it hadn't worked out the way he'd imagined it. He was alone too much and hated it. To compound the problem, Eric felt disloyal to his father when his mother's boyfriend would tell him to do things. Life was a mess. Fortunately his mother noticed his depression, and together they went to a therapist who helped work things out.

Parents' new friends and lovers can take up a lot of time, and you may feel quite resentful. You can do a couple of things to work it out. First, try to explain to your mother or father how you are feeling. They may be unaware of what you are going through. They need to keep some balance in their lives and often don't realize when one part of life takes undue precedence over another.

Sherry thought the biggest problem she had with her parents' divorce was having to accept her father's girlfriend. Although Sherry lived with her mother, she saw her father nearly every weekend. In talking about the girlfriend, Sherry said, "I don't like her. She's so stupid, she can't even carry on a conversation at the dinner table. I guess what bothers me too is that I know that they knew each other before my parents got divorced."

That's a new wrinkle. Blame. If you suspect that your parent was involved with a person before the divorce, that person can easily become a convenient target for blame as the cause of the divorce. It also makes you feel that your father or mother was deceitful and disloyal. Perhaps in that particular instance, your parent was. However, that does not necessarily make your parent a bad person. Your parent behaved badly, but almost everyone does sometime in life. Remember, too, rarely is a divorce as simple as Dad or Mom leaving for another woman or man. The causes go much deeper. The other woman or man can be better seen as the last straw rather than the whole problem.

It's pretty hard sometimes to keep the roles straight. You must see your father the parent as being separate from the man who was your mother's husband. The same goes for Mom as mother and wife. Your mom or dad may have thoroughly enjoyed being a parent and may have done a terrific job at it and yet couldn't be a good husband or wife for whatever reason. A parent has very different feelings for the children than for a husband or wife. Your mother or father can love you unconditionally and yet not love your mother or father anymore, leaving open the possibility of falling in love with another person.

In many instances your parents become worried and concerned about how you will react to their dating. They may ask themselves, "Will the kids be angry with me if I go out and leave them alone? Will they like the person I date? What if I bring my date home? What if my date stays over? How will the kids feel if I become sexually involved with this person?

How do you handle your parents' dating? The best way

you can. Accept the fact your parents need adult relationships. Try not to see their dates as replacements or as intruders in your relationship with your parents. It's not that your parents don't love you, it's just that they need something more than a parent-child relationship.

Visiting

It probably feels pretty weird to "visit" a parent. All your life you've had your parents at home where they belonged. You "visited" grandparents, friends, and crazy little cousins. You were told what to expect and exactly how to behave. This is a whole new ball game.

Remember, this visitation bit is new for them, too, and they feel unsure and ill at ease and may try overly hard to make you happy. Divorced fathers are often referred to by overwrought custodial mothers as Disneyland daddys. Weekends with Dad consist of a veritable whirl of wonderful places to go and things to see. The Disneyland daddy seems to have lots of money to spend buying things. You may have a marvelous time cashing in on this phenomenon. But then again, it may get very old very fast. What you need is a father, not a tour director. Patience. The whole scene probably gets to him, too. Balance and sanity will return, and you'll see Dad once again as you knew him.

The older you are, the more commitments of your own you may have that can interfere with your visits. John's father lived 150 miles away but often drove up to spend a day with John and his brothers. John loved his father and looked forward to seeing him. But every time his father planned a trip up, a huge soccer tournament or a smashing party would fall on the same day. Sometimes he'd just cry at the utter frustration of being pulled into two directions. Fortunately, his father was very flexible and understanding, and everything worked out fine.

If you have to go stay with your mother or father, you can really begin to resent it for other reasons.

Karen explained her problems this way: "I am living with my mom, and my dad lives about an hour away. He shares his apartment with his girlfriend, Sally. I spend every other weekend with my dad. I usually don't want to go because there is something happening home that weekend, like a party. My mother likes all of us to go to my dad's at the same time because she likes to have weekends to herself.

"Since I can't convince my parents to let me stay home, I have to go to my dad's. And, I admit, I am determined to have a bad time. And Sally, whom I hate, doesn't help the situation. It would be a lot easier if I had only one home to stay in."

Karen finally came up with a solution. She behaved so miserably that her father didn't want her to come anymore. That was one way of handling it, a very effective one at that, but there were alternatives. Maybe one weekend a month she could have cleared her calendar and gone to Dad's and been pleasant. She might have also told her father that she wanted some time with him by herself and suggested that he come to pick her up so that they could spend the day together near home without going back to his apartment for the weekend.

Her mother had a legitimate request in the situation, too. Many single mothers desperately need time to themselves without the constant responsibility of children. Karen needed to understand that from her mother's point of view. She could have arranged to stay with a friend on some occasions when her little brothers were staying with Dad.

Often you'll find that a solution to a problem will become clear when you see things from another person's perspective. When you can recognize the need behind the request or rule, you have the key to finding a workable solution.

Besides being inconvenient, having two homes and often two families can be a painful predicament. The times that were supposed to be the best of times become the worst of times. When the anger and painful feelings rage on and on between your parents, the important times in your life provide a fresh battleground for your parents and can be terribly uncomfortable for you.

While talking about the difficulties of being a divorced kid during the holidays, one sixteen-year-old girl said, "It's like, who gets me for Christmas? My parents always fight over where I'm going to be for Christmas. It's like a contest: 'Who gets Andrea this year?' I'm a prize."

Like Andrea, Michelle felt pulled apart at a point in her life when she should have been looking forward to a wonderful day. She said, "When I graduated from sixth grade, my father said he didn't want my mother to come and forbade me to tell her about it. I got really upset and cried a lot. The next day I called my mom from school, and we made a plan. She would come after the ceremony. I was scared my dad would find out, but he never did.

"When she came, she gave me a tape recorder as a present. I started to cry because I couldn't take it because then my dad would know she had come. I told her to keep it until Christmas and give it to me then. Later, when she was getting ready to leave, we sat in her car. I said, 'Why did you and Dad do this to me?' The day I graduated, it rained."

What can you do? You may feel overwhelmed and stretched to the breaking point between the two strong forces—Mom and Dad. First you've got to figure out exactly what it is *you* want. That's tricky sometimes after being bombarded by what others want from you for so long. The hard part, though, is telling each parent. A good thing to try is to use the word "I" and avoid the word "you." For example, "*I'd* like Mom to come to graduation, too. *I* know it will be hard for you, but it means a lot to *me*." That sounds much better and less antagonistic than "Mom should be able to come no matter what *you* say. *You* are really being unfair." It may work. Try it.

Can you imagine how complex a wedding can be? Who will be invited? Who will come? Where will each person sit?

What If Your Parent Lives Far Away?

Maybe you are a kid whose father or mother lives far away. After a divorce, it is not uncommon for one of the parents to move. It may be that a better job opportunity comes the parent's way or that the parent wishes to start a new life somewhere else. It doesn't mean they don't love you. This situation often makes seeing your noncustodial parent more difficult, but it can have a lot of advantages. You get trips rather than disruptions. You get to see a new part of the country. When Samantha was asked to describe divorced kids, she said, "Divorced kids are angry, frustrated, touchy, and very experienced travelers." She spent part of every other weekend on a train traveling to see her father, who lived two hundred miles away. Eric was only five when he took a plane by himself to Iowa to visit his dad for Christmas. Scott flew three times a year across the entire country to visit his father, who lived on the opposite coast.

If you live far away, you can still have a good relationship with your other parent. The telephone becomes the main connection. Do you know the song "Reach Out and Touch Someone"? Do it. It works best if you set up a time each week when you'll talk. You can really plan and look forward to enjoying vacations together.

When Parents Don't Seem to Care Anymore

Sometimes a very puzzling and painful situation can arise when it appears that one parent doesn't seem to care about his or her children anymore. A kid to whom this happens wonders if Mom or Dad didn't divorce him, too. If this happens to you, you really have to do some talking to yourself or the feeling of rejection will gnaw at you. In many cases, the parent doesn't know how to express his or her love to you. Your parent may feel ashamed or guilty and just can't reach out to you at this time. He or she feels confused, bewildered, and disconnected with the life that existed before the divorce. You were one of the many pieces in the old life. How to arrange the old familiar pieces into a new and unknown framework can really throw an adult.

If this is the case, time will help. Hang in.

Another factor may have to do with societal attitudes toward men and women. Many men have never been shown or been allowed to freely express emotions, particularly tender ones. Since they were young, they were expected to be "big boys." No matter how desperately mutilated big brother became after a tricycle accident, Dad told him, "Don't cry. Be a big boy. Big boys don't cry." But just let little sister, or big sister for that matter, take a similar spill and she got cuddled and cooed at and held and cared for until the pain stopped. Maybe that's why Dad is so distant now. He's being a big boy.

Women who leave their families also suffer from society's scorn. How could a woman leave her children? Why, it's the most basic, strongest biological instinct—motherhood. Whether anyone has actually said it or not, your mom feels it. She probably can't figure it out, either, and this leaves her desperately confused and in pain. Could this be the reason Mom seems detached and aloof?

Running Away

Sometimes the divorced parents' problems are not so temporary. If a person becomes so angry that there seems to be no way out, that person just may run away.

You've probably heard a lot recently about missing, runaway kids. Missing children hot lines have been established to help locate them. But what about a missing parent?

Why do parents run away? The most prominently mentioned reason is anger. Anger not at you but at your other parent or the situation, the lawyers, the judge—whatever. Another reason could be because they fear the responsibility of being a parent. Mothering or fathering takes tremendous commitment: time, energy, money, patience, caring. Some people can't handle it but find out too late, for their children have already been born. And then, some people are just plain selfish. They can think only of themselves. Do any of these reasons have anything to do with you? No, not one.

Who's the loser when a parent runs away? You? You bet, but the biggest loser is your runaway parent. Dawn's parents were divorced when Dawn was only two. Now, at sixteen, she remembers well growing up and looking forward to seeing her father. She said, "The thing I longed for at the age of ten was the weekends, only because that was when my father would come. After a while, his visits became fewer; I began to wait and wait, but he never came again. I'm still waiting for the day he knocks on my front door and sees me. Maybe then he will be put to shame and realize all the pain he put me through."

When you're left without a father or a mother, it's not easy to resolve the nagging question in your mind, "What's wrong with me? Am I so unlovable?" You think, perhaps that if you can find a reason within you, then you can change it and therefore change the situation.

There is absolutely nothing about you that caused Dad or Mom to disappear. Although the pain is most personal, you may feel better to know that there are many other kids out there in the same predicament, feeling the same way, wondering the same things. In fact, a recent survey of over 1,400 divorced kids found that fifty-two percent had not heard from their fathers in over a year; thirty-five and a half percent hadn't had any contact for five years. Hang on to the fact that your absent father or mother has the problem, the weakness, the inability for responsibility or commitment, the emotional block—whatever. You have a life with many people who do love and care for you and a future bright with promise for loving and being loved.

Living in a Stepfamily

When you were little, you probably read the tales or saw the film versions of *Hansel and Gretel*, *David Copperfield*, and *Cinderella*. All of them portrayed the cruel and wicked stepmother as the villain. Now contrast that image of the stepfamily to the television sitcom *The Brady Bunch*, the perfect stepfamily with no history. What are stepparents really like? What can kids expect when parents remarry?

About a million kids a year find themselves becoming part of stepfamilies. Estimates range from 8 million to 15 million kids under the age of eighteen living with a step-parent. This means that one in six kids in the United States lives in that very complex family unit, the stepfamily. Although parents and children alike generally agree that life in the single-parent family is simple—a piece of cake—compared with life in a stepfamily, moms and dads remarry at a rate of a half million marriages a year. Thirteen hundred stepfamilies with kids under eighteen are formed each day.

Usually the two people who enter into a remarriage hold the highest hopes of creating a new, wonderful, perfect family. Your parent may think that after all she's been through, after all she's learned, now at last she and her husband will have the happy family they both always wanted. Then the problems of day-to-day living in a stepfamily begin to shatter the dream. Rather than seeing yourselves as being part of a unique life-style, you may see yourselves as a poorly functioning nuclear—"regular"—family. The dynamics are different. No matter how kind, considerate, and understanding all of you normally may be, the new situation of living together places stress on everyone, and this in turn creates problems. Just as your life-style is unique, so must the solutions be.

Before you actually live in a stepfamily, you can't imagine how many things can cause problems. For one thing, there are just too many people involved. It's entirely possible to have a mother, a father, a stepmother, a stepfather, "real" brothers and sisters, stepbrothers and stepsisters, half brothers and half sisters, four "real" grandparents, and four more stepgrandparents. Can you imagine your Christmas list? You'd need a full-time job to pay for a trinket for each. With so many people now part of the family, the possibility of problems developing with one or some of them almost certainly is present.

The big problems, however, focus on the new stepparent. A very interesting phenomenon has been observed by many kids concerning the dramatic difference between the person their mother dated and the person their mother married. Greg explained it this way: "I don't like my stepfather. I used to before he married my mom, but then he changed. It was like he tried hard to make us like him while he was dating mom, but as soon as he worked his way into the family, he forgot how to be nice. It was really weird. I'm not sure about my future stepmother. She's really nice now, but I'm afraid she'll do the same." What happened to that person who took you places, bought you things, and seemed so nice? Barry described the man his mother married as a "real Jeckyll and Hyde." "Mister Nice Guy," Barry said, "quickly degenerated to a mean, intolerant bully."

Because your new parent comes into your family as a stranger, he or she is unfamiliar with your history. Usually the couple forms first and then the children come, but in a stepfamily the situation is reversed. One young man put it this way: "If your parent is remarried, you must remember that this strange man or woman is trying to pick up your life partway through, and this in itself could be an entire course."

You are unique. Sometimes a stepparent has a hard time dealing with that, especially if he or she has never had children. Your stepparent may have some pretty definite ideas about what you "should" do at your age that are in actuality pretty foreign to what you can do or are used to doing. There is an old saying that no one knows more about raising children than someone who has never had any. This statement can be painfully true and extraordinarily frustrating in a stepfamily.

However, if your stepparent has children of his own who didn't turn out too well, he will go overboard making demands on you so that you don't make the same mistakes or turn out the way the first group of children did. Or if her children are super kids, your stepmother may feel she has the formula for perfect parenting and you're next up for the plan.

In any case, you may have difficulties accepting this new person in your life. Remember that someone who feels like an outsider may try too hard or get angry and resentful.

Judy Stratton, a seventh grade student from Yorktown Heights, New York, wrote a wonderful story about the problems of accepting a stepparent. Benjamin, the stepfather in the story, is the type of stepparent who tries very hard.

Divorce Doesn't Seem So Bad, Except When It Happens to You

Hi, I'm Ally, Ally McCarthy. To my friends I'm just the average girl next door with the greatest stepfather in the world. But before I get into a detailed story about him, let me tell you about myself.

I have brown hair, brown eyes, and am four foot six. (I'm short for my age.) As you can tell, I'm not the pick of the litter.

I live with my sister, Tiffany; my mother, Cathy; and my stepfather, Benjamin, who is the problem.

Now, you don't have to start feeling sorry for me, because I am not one of those poor souls whose father died in a tragic car accident. Instead, he betrayed me and ran away with his secretary. We haven't heard from him since, except for the time he requested a divorce; it was granted, of course.

I am not intending to make you cry, so I'll get on with it. I am thirteen, and I live in Elliot Falls, Texas.

Life for me with my friends isn't a problem, and before Benjamin came, life at home wasn't that bad, either.

Why, I remember my third birthday party; there I was in my pink dress with Karen (my best friend since I was two) standing next to me and Daddy holding my hand, my dad, the dad who understood me and knew how I felt.

"Ally, Ally." That's mom calling me. I suppose it's time for dinner. Oh! Wow! Lucky me, I get to go downstairs to see Benji and Tiffany. I mean, they are so palsy-walsy, it's gross.

"Allison, dear, will you please pass the salt to me?" That's Tiffany. She is only eleven, but she acts as everybody should, as Benjamin and mom do, and they cater to her. Sometimes I wonder about her. What will she be like when she's grown up?

Well, I better do the dishes or I'll catch hell.

Anyway, anything is better than being with Benjamin. He is always trying to get me on his side by buying me presents and bending over backwards to be nice. Doesn't he know that I don't allow myself to be won over? Nobody could take the place of my dad. Even though my father is a rat, nobody or nothing could step in front of my memories of him, especially not Benjamin.

I can ask myself one question about Benjamin: "Why do my friends think he is the greatest?" That's all they are saying, things like he is so great, you are so lucky, and I bet he takes you everywhere. Maybe it's because he is always overly nice to them by volunteering to drive, complimenting them, and taking time to talk to them, which most fathers around here don't do. I can't even say anything bad about him to my friends, because right away they will contradict me.

And there is Karen Singer. She is the only friend I can really trust. She doesn't think my stepfather is great, but she doesn't think he is terrible, either. Because when she thinks of me, she doesn't think of Benjamin, she thinks of Ally McCarthy. She is always there for me to talk to and get advice from. Her usual advice is to try to get along with him. But I can't seem to push myself to do it.

You don't know how hard it is to get along with a new father after you trusted another one so much that it hurt when he left and didn't even call (which is exactly what my father did to me).

Lately, since the marriage, I have been staying in my room, as I am doing now, thinking about running away. But of course, what good would that do? It would just give me more problems.

Then there are other times I think about my dad, the father I once loved. Like one of the times we went bowling. I remember that he got his hand stuck in the bowling ball, and when he went to let it go of it, he fell. We really died laughing. (He did get it off, though.)

But of course that is in the past, and nothing can bring it back, even though I wish something could.

Maybe my mom has my dad's phone number or address, something I could use to get in touch with him. Maybe he does want to see me and just lost my phone number, or maybe he is scared to call while Benjamin is home.

But there I go, daydreaming again about things that are not true. Why is it so hard to face up to the truth?

Somewhere in me I feel that I can face the world and everything in it. But how do I start? Life is just so complicated.

Maybe I will go downstairs and *try* to talk to Benjamin.

I did it! I actually had a conversation with him, and he asked me, only me, to the ball game on Saturday. It's really not as hard as it seemed. I wonder how Saturday will turn out.

"Allison, hurry up! We are going to be late! Don't forget your mitt." He is calling me. I better get going or we really will be late.

This is the third Saturday so far that we have done something together. I keep waiting for the whole rigamarole about how he doesn't want to take the place of my father, he just wants to add to it. But it's not coming.

We have talked about small things: the game, school, friends, and Tiffany. These are the things that have concerned us during the past few weeks. Maybe it's better, because I really feel like I'm beginning to accept him.

Oh! The crowd is booing. I think the visiting team just scored, but I am not sure. I wonder if Benjamin knows. I better ask.

Ben, da, dad. I don't really need an answer to my question because the smile on his face answers anything I'll ever want to ask.

Judy portrayed her heroine as a mature young lady able to push aside fantasy and accept reality. Benjamin was a patient man who kept trying. Hurray for him and for the family! Patience and caring are usually repaid tenfold, but they sure can be hard to maintain, especially if efforts are constantly met with either no response or, worse, a negative one.

The story also opens up a most important issue: *loyalty*. Loyalty is the central issue for most kids. By accepting the stepparent, you may feel you have been disloyal to your natural parent. This feeling is very real, but objectively it is possible to love both parents.

Dr. Walter Lipow, president of Equal Rights for Fathers in New York State, explains it this way: "Loving two people is not like having a orange which you have to divide two ways; it's more like having an endless supply of water. You can just keep loving and loving, and the love will never be diminished."

It's a lot easier to say than to allow yourself to do. Sometimes, when you really do like your stepparent, you are haunted by feelings of guilt. You feel like you are disloyal to your natural parent and may shut out the stepparent even though he or she has been wonderful to you. S. W. Simon wrote in *Stepchild in the Family*, "The child sees what adults don't want to see, that a man can have a new wife, a woman a new husband, but that he, the child, cannot have a new parent. There is no such thing as an ex-mother or an ex-father."

Melanie's parents hated each other after their divorce. Melanie lived with her father, sister, and stepmother but often saw her mother, who lived nearby. She constantly worried about being with one of her parents and meeting the other parent by accident. Of course, with her parents living only a few miles apart, it happened.

As Melanie put it: "I was in the store with my mom and sister about a week before school started, getting clothes and supplies. My sister and I were looking at pens and pencils and all that stuff. My mom needed some pens, too, so she was right by my side when all at once my dad and stepmother said, 'Hi, girls.' I was in total shock because my mom and stepmother don't get along at all.

"I wondered what I should do. Should I give my step-mother a kiss or a hug? I didn't want to kiss her because I didn't want to get my mom mad, so I gave my dad a hug. So as not to make my stepmother angry, I gave her a hug, too. I figured my dad would be mad if I didn't.

"After they left, I asked my mother if she was mad at me, and she said no. I went to get some paper in the front of the store, when I saw my dad's car parked out front as if they were waiting for my sister and me. They stayed there for one minute before they left. I was so afraid to tell my mother that I got a really bad headache. I was so afraid to tell my mother that I got a really bad headache. My mom said I was sick because of the shock of seeing them in the store, but I couldn't help thinking about what my dad would say when I got home."

Melanie constantly had to deal with being caught in the middle between her two families. Her stepmother often made cruel comments about her mother, and when people laughed at them, Melanie felt deeply hurt and got really angry at her stepmother. Melanie also felt that her stepmother was particularly cruel to *her* for a reason many kids have mentioned: *She looked just like her mother*. Many kids have felt strongly that their stepmothers resented them because of the kids' marked resemblance to their natural parents. When feelings between the two are particularly raw, resentment is more apt to flare up.

Experts have also noted another phenomenon in stepparent-stepchild relationships that probably contributed to Melanie's problems as well. Stepmothers and stepdaughters as well as stepfathers and stepsons have "same-sex" problems. For some reason, children and stepparents have more of a problem when they are of the same sex. Often the oldest son, for instance, will have severe conflicts with his stepfather. The rest of the family may make it, but the strife between those two will rage on relentlessly. Similarly, the stepmother who moves into a house where a daughter has been "taking care of things," including Dad, will meet intense resistance from the stepdaughter.

The biological bond between parent and child is so strong, the feelings of loyalty so intense, that stepparents have a difficult task fitting into their stepchildren's lives. As a stepchild you face painful, confusing feelings of disloyalty; a stepparent faces other feelings just as confusing and painful. Karen Savage, a psychologist and stepmother, puts the problem this way: "However much the stepmother wishes to succeed in her ill-defined and contradictory role, she faces a wall of prejudice, false expectations, and anger that is likely to defeat her. As her goodwill turns sour in the face of repeated rejection, she often becomes what she was mythically foretold to be." You remember—the cruel and wicked stepmother of the fairy tales.

The whole stepfamily scene sounds so complicated that you may wonder if there is any way that the newly formed group can really become a family. Experts say that to become a family takes anywhere from three to seven years. They have broken down the process into three different stages.

At first the stepparent's feelings toward the children are positive. The person enters a new marriage with high hopes for a happy family and wants to love and enjoy the children.

When Robert met and fell in love with Marlene, he was just delighted at a second chance for happiness. He'd gotten divorced after twenty-five years of marriage and was lonely and missed family life. Marlene was younger and had three children: twelve-year-old Larry and twin ten-year-old daughters, Denise and Deborah. Robert had grown sons of his own and was particularly delighted with the thought of having daughters. He'd been a good father to his sons and felt that he had a lot to offer Larry, who had severe learning disabilities.

The wedding was a glamorous event. The rose garden of the huge new house Robert and Marlene had purchased bloomed profusely for the occasion. The children were the true highlight of the affair. Larry was dressed in a tuxedo as a groomsman, and Denise and Deborah were darling as twin flower girls. The new family was launched in style!

Christmas had always meant a lot to Robert, and so he planned a marvelous first Christmas for his new family. They all went to one of the most expensive restaurants in the city and then to the operetta *Hansel and Gretel*. The evening cost nearly $500. Robert looks back now and wonders about his choice of shows. He wonders if the image of Hansel and Gretel's cruel and wicked stepmother hurt his chances of being a stepfather.

Usually, in this first state, the new stepparent will deny any negative feelings about the children and smile, smile, smile.

During the second stage, the stepparent begins to recognize negative feelings but worries about the marriage, and so he or she suppresses them and ignores them.

Let's go back to Robert's new marriage and life with Larry, Denise, and Debbie. As life settled down and the aura of the romantic storybook wedding faded, it soon became quite evident to Robert that his stepchildren had a way of living that was radically different from anything he was familiar with. The mess in the house was overwhelming. He knew that the apartment they'd lived in with Marlene had been messy, but he thought that the huge new home would help. He also knew that Marlene had not disciplined the children much but understood that she found coping with a job and three children very difficult. With his love and support, certainly life for her would be better and order could be reestablished.

As the clutter reached knee level, Robert's agitation increased. After a few subtle attempts to discuss his feelings with Marlene, he opted for hiring a cleaning lady. Three times a week a maid came to clean up. By the time the weekend was over and before the maid came on Tuesday, the depth of clothes and clutter had reached its former level. Still Robert said little and tried to spend more time in his study.

The final stage in the process of becoming a family usually begins when something specific happens so that feelings come out in the open. Things can go in either of two directions. The first possibility is that things will get much worse. During this stage, the couple may openly question whether the marriage was a mistake and if it should continue. Things may get so bad that the stepparent will leave or the child will move out, choosing to live with the other natural parent or perhaps a grandparent.

Robert's situation reached this point after two and a half years. No longer could he stand living with the messy, unruly children. Fed up, he fired the maid. When he, Marlene, and the children began to discuss the conflicts involved in their daily existence, tempers blew. Larry and the girls hurled vile insults at Robert, and Marlene sat silent, pulled apart, grief-stricken at the horrible scene. Within months, battle lines were drawn: Robert versus the children. For a while Marlene walked the precarious middle line, then she ignored the whole situation, but finally she sided with the children. After all, they were her flesh and blood and Robert was not. The marriage ended, the house was sold, and the hopes and dreams of a happy, loving couple collapsed.

What does a remarriage look like from a kid's point of view? Alice had lived through a year of a really ugly divorce and still was rather shaken when even worse things seemed to happen. Her father, who had always been a terrific guy, quite suddenly moved to Philadelphia, 150 miles away. Worse yet, he now lived with a woman Alice didn't like very much. Just as Alice was finally starting to cope with that whole scene, her mother announced that she was getting married. "What is this, a race?" Alice asked herself.

Her mother had had a very bad case of the divorce "crazies." She dated many rather strange men, including Alice's teacher, who was already married. She dashed from tennis club to singles parties to support groups, desperately trying to "find herself." Now she was getting *married*!

Bill, the husband and stepfather to be, seemed like a nice

enough guy. Problem: He had custody of his two daughters, aged fifteen and seventeen. Alice was fourteen at the time, had two younger brothers, and couldn't quite picture herself being deposed from the position of oldest child. The idea of two older "sisters" made her ill. Besides, they were creeps. She knew them vaguely at school.

More problems. Alice and her family lived in a huge, expensive house. She, Tommy, and Scott each had his or her own bedrooms and the family still had a bedroom left over. However, her father wanted the money for his half of the house and demanded that it be sold. Bill offered to buy out his half. No dice. Divorce wars continue after divorce, especially with a remarriage on the horizon.

So Alice, her mother, her two little brothers, and their two English sheepdogs moved into Bill's much smaller house. What a group: Bill, Mom, the two creeps, Jeanne and Joanne, Alice, Tommy, Scott, Baron and Duchess (the sheepdogs), and—of all the luck—two pesty cats that belonged to the two creeps. When the clergyman who performed the marriage asked if anyone present knew of any reason why this man and this woman should not be joined together, Alice almost shouted, "Are you kidding! Look at this mess!" She kept quiet then but did not forever hold her peace.

Bill and Mom explained calmly that everyone would have to make compromises. Alice couldn't help but ask herself, "Why should I? What do I get out of this?"

First came the room arrangements. The creeps moved in together. Neither one was exactly pleased with that situation. Scott and Tommy got the small room. Alice got the tiny little room Bill had used as a den. Swell.

Now what? Day one, week one. The bathroom. Alice marched off in the morning to take a shower. There was already a line. Mom was drying her hair, and Bill was just finishing shaving. One creep was waiting by the door, and the other one screamed, "I'm after Joanne." Great! Maybe Alice could make it to school by lunchtime. Scott and Tommy fought and tumbled each other across the hall. "Walk the dogs, please, Alice," Mom called. Right! In my bathrobe and greasy hair, Alice thought. "Keep those dogs away from Tinkerbelle and Wendy. Cats hate dogs, you know," Joanne announced with a scowl.

"This will never work" ran through everybody's mind. Mom and Bill, however, added a hopeful, "but it has to."

It's now four years later, and believe it or not, Alice's new family has made it. Even they are amazed that it worked when they look back at how many problems they had to deal with. One of Bill's daughters moved out to live with her mother, but the rest are all happily living together. Alice made friends with Joanne. In fact, they came to feel like sisters after a while. Alice grew to appreciate Bill as a good person. Even her relationship with her mother improved, since things had settled down for her, too. Maybe she had "found herself," after all. It felt good to be part of a family— normal—again.

When your parent remarries, you have some options on how to handle it. You can figure you're the victim and fight back. You may even be successful. Many kids who have been through two divorces see themselves as being a direct or indirect cause of the second marriage's ending. Alice admitted to trying that approach. She made life miserable for everyone at home and at school. She became a real brat, belligerent and nasty to everyone. At school she cut classes and got terrible grades. Her guidance counselor thought she was screaming for attention. Maybe she felt she was getting lost in this maze of new people and new situations. Her mom and Bill were patient and stuck together. Alice finally saw that there was little chance of having things the way they used to be and decided to make the best of it.

Her stepsister Joanne played a major role in helping Alice adjust. Somehow, one day, they finally "talked." Bill and Mom had taken the boys away for a long weekend at Disney World, and Alice had decided to stay home for the weekend. Since Jeanne had already moved out, Alice and Joanne were left alone in the house together and began to talk about what had happened with Jeanne. They found they had a lot in common, feeling abandoned by a parent, "different" at school, in second place to a new spouse, and generally angry at the whole situation they had done nothing to create. Each had seen the other as an intruder. Yet they both were simply the children of divorced parents who went as part of the package in a remarriage. A new bond formed, and they became very close friends. They sort of became part of a kids' alliance to weather the storms created when two families came to live together.

Daniel's story had a different ending. He'd lived with his stepfather since he was eight years old. His real father, his stepfather, and his mother had all grown up in the same neighborhood. His mom and dad got married right after high school and had Daniel and his sister within the first four years they were together. Daniel's father deserted the family, and his mother was lucky enough to become reacquainted with Gordon, who had admired her for as long as he could remember.

They remarried, Gordon adopted the two children, and they moved away from old ties in the old neighborhood in the city. Gordon tried extremely hard to be a father to the two children. He coached soccer and went to every dance recital. He established the same firm rules he'd been brought up with. After all, he didn't want Daniel or Suzanne to turn out to be the rat their father had been. Daniel looked just like his father and was talented musically, as his dad had been. Gordon feared that Daniel's music would lead him to the miserable end his father had come to.

Daniel tried hard to live up to the standards his stepfather had set for him but always seemed to fail. He couldn't give his stepfather what he wanted from him, nor was he quite sure exactly what that was. The older Daniel got, the more pressure his stepfather put on him to give up the music and do better in school. Finally, one day after his mother left for work, his stepfather hit Daniel because he hadn't answered a question. Daniel was angry and terrified. He got to school shaken and too upset to go to class. His guidance counselor saw him and suggested a family conference. The conference was a disaster. His stepfather was enraged that Daniel had told anyone about their problems and stubbornly held to his belief that Daniel was just like his father and deserved and needed harsh discipline. His mother just cried. The next weekend Daniel flew off three thousand miles to live with his real father, whom he hadn't seen in over ten years.

The other direction the family may take at this point is to have some real lines of communication begin so that a special family can be formed. More about that later in "Good News about Stepfamilies."

Areas of Discord

The biggest problem for the new stepfamily usually centers on disciplining the children. When parents raise you from birth together, a pattern of mutual agreement emerges concerning values, expectations, and acceptable behavior. No such agreement exists in a remarriage. People have radically differing philosophies about how to bring up children and sometimes hold these beliefs as absolute truths. When two adults with different approaches marry, the potential for problems is enormous and you are at the center of it all. Add to conflicting child-rearing theories the fact that you have been living with a single parent, and the situation intensifies. While you were living with just one parent, it's likely you had adult responsibilities and a more adult relationship with that parent. Enter the stepparent. You are now expected to be a child again.

When Andrew's parents were divorced, he lived alone with his mother. His mother was young and pretty and enjoyed being single. She sold the suburban split-level house, bought a foreign sports car, and moved into a condominium. Together, Andrew and his mother whipped around the country in the little car. They divided the household tasks and then went out to do all kinds of great things. Then she met John, and they got married. John had some very definite ideas about children and how they should behave. He was a psychologist. Andrew was given a list of chores and a schedule of when to do them. To improve his grades, he was given a tutor and a specified study hour. John signed him up for soccer. Andrew hated soccer but tried his best. John signed him up for the Boy Scouts. Andrew liked craft projects, but the rest of the stuff he couldn't stand. Life was hell. His mother, thrilled at finding a wealthy man who provided more than she had dared hope for, felt that Andrew was ungrateful and unnecessarily belligerent when John spoke to him. Andrew resented all the demands on himself and felt deprived of his mother's attention. He missed their life together and wished that John had never come into the picture. Andrew was further dismayed and confused at his mother's attitude. She'd been his friend and had never gotten mad at him before. What had happened?

Part of the problem here was that John had come on like a disciplinarian. It is entirely natural to resist the stepparent's authority, particularly if a friendship has not developed first. You are much more open to responding to someone you like and admire than to someone who just gives you orders.

"What can I do?" You might well ask. You could see yourself as a victim, but you do have some options: Suggest that you all sit down together to discuss the behavior expected of you and the consequences involved. Make sure you all understand the rules, and life should be easier. But beware: Timing of the family conference is everything with such a potentially hot topic. Don't have a discussion after a blowup or when anyone is angry about something. The conference should be held in a spirit of concern, friendship, compromise, and good humor.

Another problem you can't do anything about but should be aware of is money. You probably aren't privy to this information, but you should understand that the questions of who earns it, who gives it, how it is spent, and to whom it's given place stress on your parents. If your stepfather has children of his own by a previous marriage, he still has a financial obligation to them. He may also be making alimony payments to his former wife. He may have real conflicts about where his money should go. Your mom may also begin to resent the huge amount of the family income sent out each month to another family. If your mother works, she may have a hard time not seeing the money sent as her money. Your mother may also guard the support money sent by your dad to be used only for you, whereas your stepfather may feel that part of that money should go to the regular household expenses since you're part of the household. As you can see, the whole thing is very complicated and fraught with emotional overtones.

Although most money issues are dealt with by your parent and stepparent, sometimes you can be directly affected. During Steve's first year of college, his stepbrother got arrested and put in jail in a foreign country. His stepmother went crazy, trying everything to get her son released. Steve's father did his best to help. The mess cost a great deal of money, running into thousands of dollars. Steve's father didn't send Steve what he'd said he would each month at college, and each time Steve called, his stepmother would complain to him about how much money the call cost and how little money they had. Finally, Steve stopped calling and cut way back on his spending. Then his father got mad because Steve never called except when he needed something. The best thing you can do about the money problem is to stay out of it as much as possible.

Stepbrothers and Stepsisters

Another big change in your life after a remarriage can be the introduction of stepbrothers and stepsisters as part of the package. Your first visit with the new group can feel like your first day in a new school or the first night at sleep-away camp. You wonder, "What are these kids going to be like? Will they like me? Will I like them?" Besides all those questions you'd ask yourself about any new acquaintances, these kids present further problems. For instance, you may see them as rivals for your parent's attention. One kid put it this way after his stepfather's kids had spent a vacation with them: "It's hard enough sharing your room and your things, but when you have to share your parent, too, then it becomes too much."

Some kids notice a big difference in the way a stepparent treats them as opposed to the stepparent's own children. Danielle really liked her stepsister, Karen. They were exactly the same age and had a lot of things in common. When Karen came to live with them for the summer, Danielle was delighted. She took her to lots of parties and introduced her to all her friends. However, Danielle was confused and hurt by the difference between how her stepfather treated her and how he treated Karen. "When he'd come up to wake us in the morning," said Danielle, "he'd say, 'Come on, darling, it's time to get up, sweetheart,' to Karen and give her a kiss. Then he'd say as he left the room, 'Get up, Danielle.'"

"My mother felt sorry for Karen, too," Danielle went on. "Karen's got big problems, and my mom worries about her a lot of the time she's here. I guess I got jealous even as much as I liked Karen."

What about the arrival on the scene of a half brother or half sister? Often the baby's birth can bring the family together in a way that had not been possible before. As Sandy said, "My mother and stepdad just had a child fifteen months ago, and since then we all have become much closer, and now it's like we have something in common. Now we all are part of a family. Now my stepdad and I have something we can share."

Sometimes, though, if a child is born after you're a teenager, you may feel detached and strange. You may feel more like an aunt or uncle than a sister or brother. Also, you may resent all the attention the new baby receives at a point in your own life when you'd like recognition and support for some major accomplishments in growing up. For instance, you may feel that making the varsity swim team is more noteworthy than the new baby's first dip in the pool.

No one ever said it was going to be easy, but who could have guessed that life would be so complicated.

The Good News about Stepfamilies

When asked the question, "What is the best thing about living in a stepfamily?" kids came up with a list.

Money is usually the first thing mentioned. The addition of a second income can be a welcome relief to a financially stressed family. On the same theme, they mention having multiple holiday and birthday celebrations, getting more gifts, and being spoiled by eager stepparents as big pluses.

An even bigger plus is having your parent happy again. Seeing marriage as producing a happy, secure way to live may also restore your own hopes for a happy marriage. Since your parent is happier, you have a much better chance of having a good relationship with him or her. Diane said, "I have gained a better relationship with my mom. We can talk and have time together. We never used to be able to do that because she was usually mad and upset and would just go to sleep after a fight."

There is also good news about all the "steps." Your stepparent can really turn out to be a good friend. Because a stepparent isn't your real parent, he or she can be more objective and can serve as your advocate with your own parent. After a discussion at the dinner table one night with her mother, which ended with them disagreeing, Eileen turned to her stepdad, John, and said, "You know, John, I think we married the wrong person." They all laughed.

Your stepbrothers and stepsisters may turn out to be great friends. In fact, some of these relationships go on after a second divorce. Many of the "steps" provide the possibilities of more people to depend on and more people to like. It can be a really enriching experience because you've added new people to your life whom you'll find have special strengths you can count on and learn from.

You have an edge on kids who've never been through what you have because you've seen and experienced different life-styles. You've therefore acquired more options for your own life in the future. You have learned how to be flexible and understanding and how to accept change— an important lesson in a complex world.

Cynthia has a unique family. She lives with her father, brother, and sister; her stepmother, stepbrother, and stepsister; and a half brother.

She carefully thought about the question of what she'd gained as a child of divorce and said, "I believe I have gained the love of two families. It just means to me that I have a big family, not a split one. I have gained a bigger and better family. Two families are better than one in some cases. You get more love, more support, and lots of people who care about you. I love everyone the same, and in our family there are no 'steps.'"

Different Life-styles

> The family in its old sense is disappearing from our land,
> and not only our free institutions are threatened, but the
> very existence of our society is endangered.

Where do you suppose a quote like that came from? It sounds
like a worried response to the growing problem of divorce
in the 1980s, doesn't it? Well, that fearful prophecy of things
to come was printed in the *Boston Quarterly Review* in 1859!

The American family has always been changing. Although
television commercials would have you believe that a family
is made up of a father, a mother, two kids, and one dog,
you know better. But sometimes kids feel different, strange,
embarrassed, or guilty when their homes don't match up
with what they've been told is "normal." When parents
divorce, the family certainly changes, sometimes dramati-
cally.

Your family may be one of those unique forms which exist but are hardly ever seen on television.

Living with Grandparents

If your parents divorced when they were young and you were very young, your mother or father might have moved back home. Now, with three generations under one roof, you've created not a new-style family but one that traditionally existed from the beginning of time. Everyone needs and depends on everyone else. Your grandmother probably baby-sat for you while your mother went out to work to bring money into the home. Your fondest memories probably center on the little things you did with your grandparents: planting the garden with Grandpa, reading stories with Grandma. In that regard, you were a very lucky kid. Few kids today get to really know their grandparents.

Maybe your grandparents don't understand why you wear your hair that way or why on earth you go out looking like that, but that generation gap is to be expected. You can handle it.

Rachel's mother divorced her father when Rachel was only an infant. Her mother was only twenty at the time and could not afford to live on her own with a tiny baby. Reluctantly she moved back to the big family home. In thinking back on how the divorce affected her life, Rachel said, "I never felt pain over my parents' divorce. I was too young to remember my father at all. I like the fact that my parents divorced when I was so young because it kept me from hurting so much. I also am kind of glad my parents divorced, in a way, because it brought my mother and me a lot closer since I am her only child. The divorce also brought me and my grandparents and their children—my aunts and uncles—closer, since we all lived in the same house. Living with them made up for me not having a father."

Being Separated from Brothers and Sisters

"Being separated from my sister was a lot worse for me than being separated from my mother," explained Chris. "You know, we played together, grew up together. I worry a lot about her and how she's doing. It's hard."

For whatever reasons, sometimes sisters and brothers go with different parents in a divorce. The reasons aren't important, but the feelings you have about the whole thing are. The longing for the absent brother or sister hurts deeply, especially if you were close. Mary, however, didn't realize how much she loved her brother until he'd moved out to live with his father. After talking about the lack of money, the overwhelming responsibilities in caring for her baby sister, and her dislike for her father's new wife, Mary said, "Still, the worst thing was being separated from my brother."

You'll have to try extra hard to stay close to your absent brother or sister. Plan vacations together, talk on the phone, send funny cards and letters. Most important, *tell* your brother or sister how you feel. It will make him or her feel better and will help your brother or sister understand how important he or she is to you.

Changing Custody

Kristine came out of her lawyer's office stunned and disbelieving. The whole process of getting a divorce was nerve-wracking enough, but this one item of counsel she'd heard that day would hang over her head for more than ten years. Her lawyer told her to expect that when her three boys turned thirteen or fourteen, they might choose to go live with their father. He explained that in the normal process of adolescents seeking independence from the mother, divorced kids had an actual place to go. She never forgot that warning although all three of her sons lived with her until they went off to college.

A substantial number of kids, particularly boys, do decide that they'd rather live with the other parent at some point during their growing-up years. You know the old story: The grass is always greener on the other side of the fence. Some believe that their lives will improve: Things just have to be better at Dad's rather than here having to do all this stuff. Mom will be so glad to see me, she'll treat me better, and I won't have to cook and do laundry anymore.

Sometimes it works out well, and other times the change lasts only for a matter of months and then it's back home again.

Jason didn't get the chance to make the decision to move, he got moved. When he boarded the plane the summer before eighth grade to visit his father, he had no idea he wasn't coming back. Unbeknownst to him, his mother had decided she couldn't handle him anymore. She was going through a second divorce and had a toddler to worry about as well as Jason's two younger sisters. He'd seen his father only a few weeks every other summer since he was six, and so he already felt uncomfortable about the visit. To complicate matters further, his father had just remarried for the third time to a woman Jason had never met who had two daughters of her own.

It wasn't until Jason began to ask questions about his flight home that his father told him that he wasn't going home. He felt betrayed and became enraged with both parents for the deception. All he thought about for the next six months was his home on the West Coast. He desperately missed his mother, his brother and sisters, his dog, and his friends. He hadn't even said good-bye.

In the aftermath of the divorce, the fallout may cause many terrible, unfair things to happen to you over which you have no control. All you can do is keep trying to take care of yourself. Hold on to the fact that you will have an independent life someday in which you can better control the things that happen to you. Plan for that day by doing your best in school, making good friends, and developing the talents you have.

Growing Up with Neither Parent

The 1981 census found that an incredible 2,295,000 kids live with neither parent. Of these children, 886,000 are under six, 893,000 are between six and fourteen, and another 517,000 are between fifteen and seventeen.

Little is known about them. Other than the obvious reason of being an orphan, how do such a large number of kids find themselves growing up with neither parent?

Although Brad would not be counted among that number because his mother lived in the same house, he truly did bring himself up. Overwhelmed with the responsibility of five young children, no job, and no job skills, Brad's mother turned to drugs and alcohol. Her retreat from responsibility reached the point where she finally built herself a room in the basement in which to live. The kids got the upstairs, which she rarely entered other than to bring some groceries each week. Brad was the oldest of the five children and the only one to successfully overcome the neglect they all suffered. Fortunately, he was extremely intelligent and used his intellect to help surmount his problems. He did very well in school, graduating in the top ten percent of his high school class and scoring over 1,400 (a very fine score) on his college S.A.T.'s. A top engineering school offered him enough of a scholarship to begin college. He studied extremely hard, knowing that his continuation in school depended wholly on scholarship aid. After the first semester he had a 3.8 average, nearly all A's.

Brad is a survivor. When things got too rough at home, he often spent the night with friends. He didn't freeload, though; each morning he'd get up and fix the whole family a huge breakfast in repayment for their hospitality.

Through using the best of what he had—intelligence, a sense of humor, and talent—he's now on his way to a very successful life. His strength of character and survival instincts will equip him well for the future.

Diana and Jeremy could be counted among the 2,295,000 kids living with neither parent. Diana and Jeremy are brother and sister. The marriage between their father and mother seemed doomed from the beginning. Their mother suffered from periods of depression and anxiety, and their father could not cope well with his wife's problems. They divorced when the children were very young, and then their father disappeared. No one knew where he'd gone.

One day Jeremy came home from school to find that his mother had committed suicide. The two young children were taken in by an aunt and uncle, who brought them up.

Jeremy found a nice group of friends in the new town and did very well in school. Although the new "parents" were strict, he enjoyed being part of a normal home. Diana did well until junior high. Then, for some reason, all the pain of having lived through so much surfaced. She felt angry and resented her "parents'" strict rules. She started to become depressed, which scared her since she knew that her mother had suffered from depression. The more she rebelled, the more rigid and demanding her "parents" became until Diana ran away.

She was quickly found and got needed therapy from a competent psychiatrist.

Some people have some kind of inner strength, as Jason and Jeremy did, but others need help in coping with the big problems of life. Diana's doctor feels that it will take time but that she will be fine.

If you need help, get it. A good psychiatrist can be the best thing for you and will help you feel good about life again.

Live-In Lovers

It's not at all unusual in the years after divorce to have your family include your mother's boyfriend or your father's girlfriend. It's sort of like having a stepparent, but not completely. This person has no legal relationship with your parent, and so the arrangement may seem to have less permanence about it. Sometimes the new person can be a terrific asset; at other times he or she can be the source of tremendous problems.

Michael felt that living with his mother's boyfriend was the worst of all the problems he'd faced since the divorce. The man moved in after dating his mother for a year and has been living with the family for five years. Michael said, "Ken just lost his job at a computer company and is now selling insurance, which he hates. For the last few months he's been a real pain. He used to be cool and a very nice guy, but now he's always mad and depressed because of his job, I guess. He doesn't give a damn about us. I really did like him a lot and at one point knew him better than my own father, but now I hate him. I don't care about him and get really angry at him sometimes. I tell him to keep the hell away from me and get out of the house and never come back. I'm not sure if I even want to live around him. I might ask my dad if I can live with him because Ken is such a jerk."

Where once Ken had been Michael's friend, he became the biggest problem in his life. When the anger broke out into bitter verbal fights, Michael's mother didn't know what to do. She understood Ken's unhappiness and frustration but also felt that Michael shouldn't have to suffer for it. She felt pulled apart since she loved them both.

If you don't get along with the live-in lover, life becomes tense for everyone. You may feel that the guy's an outsider and that your mother should be on your side. After all, she is your mother. The man or woman may feel like an outsider and be insecure about having a place in this group. And your parent feels constantly in conflict between two people he or she loves.

It's a bad scene all around. Check out the section about stepparents in this book to see if there may be some ideas there for helping to smooth out your family life.

There's another side to the live-in lover picture that is positive. Jamie enjoyed living with his mother and her boyfriend very much. His mother's boyfriend has been living with them for eight years, all the way through Jamie's years in high school and college. Art, the boyfriend, got Jamie interested in biking, which became a great love of his. The three of them—Art, Jamie, and his mother—have biked in England and have big plans to cycle the Alps after Jamie's graduation from college. Art is a quiet and unassuming young artist and never got into the disciplinarian role at all. He and Jamie had a mutual respect for each other and liked each other very much.

This type of family can work out well for everyone if all the people involved respect one another and try to understand one another's needs—just the same as in any good family.

Living with a Gay Parent

The perfect family was falling apart. Mom had been the president of the PTA and active in the Girl Scouts and even was a den mother. Dad coached a kids' sport each season and earned a most adequate salary. They had a girl named Suzi and a boy named Peter. When Suzi was fifteen and Peter was thirteen, their parents began to fight with a fury that devastated them all. Finally, after months of screaming scenes, the parents announced that they were getting a divorce. Suzi and Peter felt hurt and couldn't believe it was happening. What could be worse?

But in a way the worst was yet to come. A month or so after the divorce announcement, their mother took them each aside and told them that she was a lesbian. Suzi screamed, "No, you aren't. You couldn't be!" and flew into her room. She thought that the headache she had would never go away. What would she ever tell her friends?

"Gay? You're gay?" cried Peter. Later, when his mother pressed him about how he felt about things, he said, "I'm ashamed for you."

"No, you're not," said his mother. "You're ashamed for yourself."

Since the worst thing you can call someone in junior high is "gay," the whole thing hit Peter very hard. He was embarrassed, ashamed, and disgusted and lived in fear that his friends would find out.

It took a few months, but both Suzi and Peter finally gained a sense of perspective about their mother's homosexuality. After the shock wore off, they realized that they loved their mother very much. After all, she was the same person. Patiently, their mother weathered their initial anger and agonized over their reactions. Suzi and Peter now live with their dad. Their mother felt that she needed a private life and wanted Suzi to finish high school with the kids she'd grown up with. Their mother lives close by and sees them often.

Only ten to twenty percent of all people are gay, and so few kids ever have to face this problem. In the past, courts almost automatically granted custody to the nongay parent in a contested custody hearing. They would remove children from the mother's home if she was found to be a lesbian after the divorce. However, things are changing. More and more lesbian mothers have kept their children and have been good mothers.

Besides dealing with the divorce, which is difficult, and the knowledge that one parent is gay, which can be painful, children in this situation may have to deal with two more problems. First, they must deal with the question in their minds, "Is being gay hereditary?" Will they too be gay? Second, they must decide how to handle it with their friends.

Having a parent who is gay does not mean that the children will be gay. What it does mean is that kids learn firsthand about the varieties of relationships open to people and about different forms of love.

Telling or not telling friends has to be an individual decision. Suzi and Peter handled it by doing neither. They neither explained their mother's homosexuality nor made any attempt to hide it from their friends. If Mom came around with her female lover when either Suzi or Peter had friends over, they introduced her as Mom's friend. Their friends, if they suspected anything, never mentioned it.

If you find yourself in this situation, remember that your mother or father is the same person despite this new knowledge. Try to be happy for your parent that he or she has found a way to feel fulfilled and happy. Admire your parent's courage to finally be fully who he or she is.

The Future

Worrisome stories about children from "broken" homes can really freak you if you let them. Because a kid who's been through a divorce has had a pretty chaotic time, some people expect the kid to be troubled. You know—the whole terrible scene. They figure kids from broken homes will get into drugs and alcohol, run round with a tough crowd, become destructive, and do poorly in school. Sometimes things like this happen to kids from "normal" families, too. What it all comes down to is this: You determine your future, no one else—including your parents.

A divorce is a pretty bad thing to have happen. It makes your life complicated and difficult in many ways. However, much of life consists of making the best of a bad situation, and many people are a lot worse off than you are. Rather than let rural poverty overwhelm and defeat her, Dolly Parton became a fabulously wealthy entertainer. President

Franklin D. Roosevelt had polio yet was an extremely effective leader. Jackie Robinson overcame the racial discrimination of his time to become the first black major league baseball player. Instead of being paralyzed by their limitations, these individuals looked to their possibilities.

Not too long ago a major government research project came up with some findings that surprised a lot of people who had always felt that divorce traumatized children and hurt their development. Here's the good news.

First, children under twelve who live with a divorced mother do better on achievement tests and have fewer school problems than kids from intact families. The researchers speculated that the reason was that divorced parents watch over their children more closely. That's a pretty significant speculation. It seems that single moms care a great deal for their children and carefully monitor their studies. They make sure their kids are behaving in school and doing well. Dr. Thomas Langner, a Columbia University professor, even found that divorced kids do better on IQ tests. Hurray, moms; bravo, kids.

The study also found that children between twelve and sixteen who live with quarreling parents are one and one-half times as likely to lie, bully other kids, and generally be troublesome to other kids than children living with a divorced parent. Once the fighting is over at home, kids feel less like fighting with others. Peace is catching!

Here's a kind of crazy yet interesting finding: Adults whose parents were divorced are arrested *half* as often as adults from intact families. It seems that when divorced kids grow up, they get in "less trouble and work harder," Dr. Langner says. "They don't take as many chances."

It's all in how you look at things. An old cliché but often spoken because of its inherent truth. Look at how well other divorced kids have done. See how well they learned from their experiences.

Rather than looking at your home as being broken, you might better see it as an advantage to have two homes to grow up in. As Pam said, "Some people think it's a disadvantage to have divorced parents, but I think it's an advantage. I have two lives. When I want to escape from one of my lives, I have some other place to go. Other kids can only go to their rooms, slam the door, and turn up the stereo.

"I see this as a plus because I can get two different perspectives on my life."

You also have two different models for possible lifestyles for yourself when you marry. When you are intimately a part of two homes, you understand that you have different options for ways to live. For instance, when Jerry's parents got divorced when he was five, their two lives went in entirely different directions. His dad became a top executive with an international company and traveled a great deal. When Jerry visited him, they ate in the finest restaurants, were chauffeured everywhere, and stayed in exclusive hotels or in his dad's penthouse apartment. His father's rather jet-set style of living contrasted sharply with the way he and his mother lived. They had a little cabin in the woods that they heated with wood. When they vacationed together, they went camping or on long bicycle tours. Jerry really enjoyed sort of living off the land but also got a big thrill out of the trips with his father. He's twenty-one and will soon graduate from a top Ivy League school. It'll be interesting to see what kind of life he'll lead as an adult.

What if one of your parents abandoned you? Fight off the feelings of anger and rejection and look instead at the

fact that one parent loved you so much that he or she brought
you up alone. That parent overcame the feelings of anger
and rejection to provide you with a good life. He or she
had half the time, half the money, and twice the responsibilities—but look how well you've turned out already,
and you're not finished yet. Kathy, whose father abandoned
her family when she was only two months old, defined the
ideal family as being something like hers. She lived with
her grandparents, her mother, and two older sisters. Kathy
went on, "It's not who is in the family, even though ours
is large. We are all very close. Everybody really is always
concerned about what the others are doing or where they
are. My mom always says, 'I say no because I care.' I
believe it."

In responding to the statement "After kids get adjusted
to it, having divorced parents can mean a lot of advantages
for kids" in the questionnaire found at the end of this book,
sixty percent of the kids agreed. If your parents have recently
separated, you probably still find that extremely hard to
believe. What advantages could there possibly be? Some of
the advantages fall into the tangible areas, such as receiving
more gifts, having more vacations, and acquiring more
friends.

However, the most often mentioned advantages fall into
another area. Invariably kids feel that they have really grown
as people. They feel more mature than many of their friends
who have "normal" families. Lynne said, "I learned a lot
about relying on myself and not bothering my parent about
every little thing." Sue said, "I have more freedom and
more responsibility, more feelings, more privacy, more people who depend on me, and I am allowed to make decisions
for myself." Maria felt she'd "gained a life in reality." What

does that mean? John explained it this way: "Divorced kids are better able to cope with all kinds of problems—even huge ones. Other kids have a tiny little problem—like a sprained thumb—and they see that as a tremendous problem."

You have had to examine so many things in life that you've gained a deeper understanding of yourself. You've had to draw on some strengths others aren't even aware of, and you have probably become more compassionate and understanding of other people as well. You've come a long way in growing up.

Most people of any age have a hard time dealing with change. Yet here you are, a kid, having lived through major, life-altering changes and come through. You've had to learn to be flexible. Many, many adults never achieve flexibility and suffer anxiety and fear over new things throughout their lives. Hang on to the lessons you've learned so young and life will be less awesome and more bright with promise.

As a young woman you have learned the importance of having a career. Watching your mother or your divorced friend's mother have to struggle to make a living—very often without marketable skills or recent work experience after a divorce—can make you very much aware of the need to find a vocation, a good job, a career with many opportunities. You clearly see the need to be able to support yourself and not be as dependent on a man as women of previous generations often were. A marriage is not necessarily a happy ending to your life as a single woman. Think of the new sense of self-worth your mother had as she established herself after the divorce. If you find that sense of yourself through a satisfying career and independent lifestyle, you'll probably make a better choice of partner, too.

You won't look for someone to complete your life, which means there is something lacking, but someone to add something wonderful to an already fine life.

As a young man you have learned that you have deep feelings; this is an understanding a lot of men your father's age either don't know or can't manage very well. You have experienced fear, anger, guilt, and happiness and understand that it's all right to have these feelings and express them. Did you ever notice how the football players who win the Super Bowl react and behave? They jump around screaming and crying and sort of go crazy. How about the losers? It's okay to cry and be sad. Many adult men seem to be afraid to let their true feelings show. Sometimes they are afraid to even admit they have these very deep and intense feelings. You have had them all and learned that it's perfectly normal to have them, use them, learn from them, and share them with other people—especially those people who are in the same boat.

When you look ahead to the future, you have a great store of experiences and well-learned lessons to fall back on.

You probably look forward to getting married yourself someday. Most kids feel that even though their parents were divorced, they still want to get married. They also believe that they've learned a lot about marriage and will work harder at it than their parents did because they know how many people get hurt in a divorce. You are probably less naive than many other people are about marriage because you are aware that there is no such thing as a perfect family. Greg wrote that "a perfect family only exists on TV and in people's minds."

Nearly all divorced kids agree that one lesson they have learned is to be more careful in choosing a partner—both when and who. Many kids feel that their parents married too young and feel that had they waited until they were older and more mature, they would have chosen a more suitable partner for a lifetime together. Most divorced kids are optimistic about a happy married life.

You can face life confident that you are a strong person and are capable of handling what life brings. Your parents' divorce probably shaped your life more than any other single event. However, that is not to say it ruined your life, just changed it.

When Jerry, the kid with a jet-set dad and a pioneer mom, had to write an essay for a college application on a significant life-changing event, he chose his parents' divorce. After carefully thinking it through, he said, "But I can't imagine being any different than I am." That's a good point. You adjust, learn, and become the best person you can be within the life you have. You have survived an incredibly difficult time in your life. *You are a new person, a different person, a better person*. You are great!

Questionnaire

The following questionnaire has been answered by 206 kids, 57 parents, and 26 grandparents.

You may find it very interesting to answer it yourself and compare your responses with those of other people who have experienced divorce. It's very easy and takes only a few minutes.

Circle the response that best describes your feelings about the following statements. There are no right or wrong answers.

SA: strongly agree
A: agree
U: undecided
D: disagree
SD: strongly disagree

1. Divorce is usually harder on the kids than on the parents. SA A U D SD

2. Divorce has no effect on grandparents. SA A U D SD

3. It is better for parents to let kids know that they are going to get a divorce before they separate. SA A U D SD

4. Parents should attempt to hide their feelings about the divorce from the kids.   SA   A   U   D   SD

5. Parents should be friendly with each other after a divorce.   SA   A   U   D   SD

6. You can expect a kid to have problems in school when his or her parents are getting a divorce.   SA   A   U   D   SD

7. Falling out of love with a spouse isn't a good reason for a parent to get a divorce if there are kids involved.   SA   A   U   D   SD

8. Kids should not be asked questions by one parent about the other parent.   SA   A   U   D   SD

9. It is not right for grandparents to talk about divorce to their grandchildren.   SA   A   U   D   SD

10. Unless there is something very wrong with the mother, she should be assumed to be the better parent for the kid to live with.   SA   A   U   D   SD

11. It is vital for kids to have two parents who both love them.   SA   A   U   D   SD

12. Kids should try to make up their minds about which parent they want to side with during a divorce.   SA   A   U   D   SD

13. There's a fair chance that parents who divorce will get remarried to each other.   SA   A   U   D   SD

14. Parents should wait about a year or two after a divorce before dating other people.   SA   A   U   D   SD

15. Kids have a right to see the parent with whom they are not living at least once a week.   SA A U D SD

16. Mothers should remarry so that kids can have a father.   SA A U D SD

17. The parent you live with is always going to be stricter than the one you visit.   SA A U D SD

18. All children of divorced families should be allowed to see all sets of grandparents on some of the major holidays.   SA A U D SD

19. After kids get adjusted to it, having divorced parents can mean a lot of advantages for kids.   SA A U D SD

20. It is all right for divorcing parents to argue in front of their kids.   SA A U D SD

21. Most kids in school look down on or feel sorry for kids whose parents are divorced.   SA A U D SD

22. Parents should wait until their kids are teenagers before they divorce because then it's easier on the kids.   SA A U D SD

23. The reason parents divorce is usually because their kids have been a problem.   SA A U D SD

24. It is very difficult to really talk about the feelings inside yourself about your parents' separation.   SA A U D SD

25. Stepfathers and stepmothers are difficult to live with no matter how hard they try.   SA A U D SD

26. Kids' biggest worry is that they may be abandoned by the parent they're living with.   SA A U D SD

27. Kids of divorced parents often feel like running away from home.   SA A U D SD

28. Grandparents have the legal right to see their grandchildren a certain number of times per calendar year.   SA A U D SD

29. Kids whose parents are divorced are often more dependable and responsible.   SA A U D SD

30. Teachers should not be as hard on divorced kids on the first day back after a weekend or long holiday.   SA A U D SD

31. Grandparents shouldn't ask the grandchildren questions about the divorce of their parents.   SA A U D SD

32. Kids whose parents are divorced are less likely to have big problems in their own marriages when they are adults.   SA A U D SD

33. It's okay for kids to have two different systems of discipline in two different households.   SA A U D SD

34. It is not right for divorcing parents to argue in front of their children.   SA A U D SD

35. Grandchildren should frequently keep in touch with their grandparents by visiting, telephoning, or writing.   SA A U D SD

36. Kids over twelve years old should
not have to decide which parent
they want to live with.   SA   A   U   D   SD

37. Parents should not have to wait
a year or two after a divorce
before dating other people.   SA   A   U   D   SD

38. Fathers should remarry so that
the kids can have a mother.   SA   A   U   D   SD

39. Parents should stay together for
the sake of the children.   SA   A   U   D   SD

40. A teenager should have the right
to visit any grandparent or step-
grandparent during the year.   SA   A   U   D   SD

Questionnaire Results

The "Single" category refers to all students who answered this questionnaire who live with either their mother who is a single parent or their father who is a single parent.

The "Step" category refers to all students who answered this questionnaire who live with either a stepmother or a stepfather.

The "Parents" category refers to separated, divorced, or remarried parents.

The "Grandparents" category refers to people whose children (not grandchildren) are separated, divorced, or remarried.

To simplify the results, the categories of "strongly agree" and "agree" have been combined, as have the categories "strongly disagree" and "disagree."

1. Divorce is usually harder on the kids than on the parents.

29% of single parents agree   51% of parents agree
53% of stepkids agree   80% of grandparents agree

2. Divorce has no effect on grandparents.

   5% of single-parent kids   0% of parents agree
       agree   0% of grandparents agree
   13% of stepparent kids agree

3. It is better for parents to let kids know that they are going to get a divorce before they separate.

   80% of single-parent kids   92.5% of parents agree
       agree   71% of grandparents agree
   79% of stepparent kids agree

4. Parents should attempt to hide their feelings about the divorce from the kids.

   11% of single-parent kids   2% of parents agree
       agree   38% of grandparents agree
    4% of stepparent kids agree

5. Parents should be friendly with each other after a divorce.

   65% of single-parent kids   69% of parents agree
       agree   76% of grandparents agree
   77% of stepparent kids agree

6. You can expect a kid to have problems in school when his or her parents are getting a divorce.

   65% of single-parent kids   76% of parents agree
       agree   81% of grandparents agree
   72% of stepparent kids agree

7. Falling out of love with a spouse isn't a good reason for a parent to get a divorce if there are kids involved.

   17% of single-parent kids   21% of parents agree
       agree   43% of grandparents agree
   11% of stepparent kids agree

8. Kids should not be asked questions by one parent about the other parent.

96% of single-parent kids   87% of parents agree
   agree   90% of grandparents agree
99% of stepparent kids agree

9. It is not right for grandparents to talk about divorce to their grandchildren.

   11% of single-parent kids   20% of parents agree
      agree   52% of grandparents agree
   17% of stepparent kids agree

10. Unless there is something very wrong with the mother, she should be assumed to be the better parent for the kid to live with.

   13% of single-parent kids   43% of parents agree
      agree   72% of grandparents agree
   20% of stepparent kids agree

11. It is vital for kids to have two parents who both love them.

   67% of single-parent kids   91% of parents agree
      agree   91% of grandparents agree
   81% of stepparent kids agree

12. Kids should try to make up their minds about which parent they want to side with during a divorce.

   44% of single-parent kids   13% of parents agree
      agree   9% of grandparents agree
   21% of stepparent kids agree

13. There's a fair chance that parents who divorce will get remarried to each other.

   21% of single-parent kids   6% of parents agree
      agree   19% of grandparents agree
   9% of stepparent kids agree

14. Parents should wait about a year or two after a divorce before dating other people.

4% of single-parent kids agree

26% of parents agree
33% of grandparents agree

7% of stepparent kids agree

15. Kids have a right to see the parent with whom they are not living at least once a week.

85% of single-parent kids agree

75% of parents agree
81% of grandparents agree

83% of stepparent kids agree

16. Mothers should remarry so that kids can have a father.

8% of single-parent kids agree

2% of parents agree
10% of grandparents agree

17% of stepparent kids agree

17. The parent you live with is always going to be stricter than the one you visit.

60% of single-parent kids agree

67% of parents agree
59% of grandparents agree

43% of stepparent kids agree

18. All children of divorced families should be allowed to see all sets of grandparents on some of the major holidays.

83% of single-parent kids agree

87% of parents agree
86% of grandparents agree

89% of stepparent kids agree

19. After kids get adjusted to it, having divorced parents can mean a lot of advantages for kids.

60% of single-parent kids agree

50% of parents agree
29% of grandparents agree

36% of stepparent kids agree

20. It is all right for divorcing parents to argue in front of their kids.

19% of single-parent kids agree

26% of parents agree
5% of grandparents agree

15% of stepparent kids agree

21. Most kids in school look down on or feel sorry for kids whose parents are divorced.

    21% of single-parent kids agree
    20% of stepparent kids agree
    48% of parents agree
    24% grandparents agree

22. Parents should wait until their kids are teenagers before they divorce because then it's easier on the kids.

    13% of single-parent kids agree
    15% of stepparent kids agree
    6% of parents agree
    19% of grandparents agree

23. The reason parents divorce is usually because their kids have been a problem.

    3% of single-parent kids agree
    2% of stepparent kids agree
    0% of parents agree
    5% of grandparents agree

24. It is very difficult to really talk about the feelings inside yourself about your parents' separation.

    44% of single-parent kids agree
    57% of stepparent kids agree
    78% of parents agree
    62% of grandparents agree

25. Stepfathers and stepmothers are difficult to live with no matter how hard they try.

    38% of single-parent kids agree
    42% of stepparent kids agree
    46% of parents agree
    33% of grandparents agree

26. Kids' biggest worry is that they may be abandoned by the parent they're living with.

    19% of single-parent kids agree
    28% of stepparent kids agree
    72% of parents agree
    48% of grandparents agree

27. Kids of divorced parents often feel like running away from home.

50% of single-parent kids   74% of parents agree
   agree   67% of grandparents agree
40% of stepparent kids agree

28. Grandparents have the legal right to see their grandchildren a certain number of times per calendar year.

62% of single-parent kids   50% of parents agree
   agree   71% of grandparents agree
64% of stepparent kids agree

29. Kids whose parents are divorced are often more dependable and responsible.

46% of single-parent kids   56% of parents agree
   agree   43% of grandparents agree
58% of stepparent kids agree

30. Teachers should not be as hard on divorced kids on the first day back after a weekend or long holiday.

21% of single-parent kids   67% of parents agree
   agree   53% of grandparents agree
34% of stepparent kids agree

31. Grandparents shouldn't ask the grandchildren questions about the divorce of their parents.

52% of single-parent kids   72% of parents agree
   agree   86% of grandparents agree
51% of stepparent kids agree

32. Kids whose parents are divorced are less likely to have big problems in their own marriages when they are adults.

38% of single-parent kids   13% of parents agree
   agree   9% of grandparents agree
45% of stepparent kids agree

33. It's okay for kids to have two different systems of discipline in two different households.

37% of single-parent kids agree   37% of parents agree
49% of stepparent kids agree   33% of grandparents agree

34. It is not right for divorcing parents to argue in front of their children.

67% of single-parent kids agree   56% of parents agree
74% of stepparent kids agree   89% of grandparents agree

35. Grandchildren should frequently keep in touch with their grandparents by visiting, telephoning, or writing.

77% of single-parent kids agree   84% of parents agree
91% of stepparent kids agree   100% of grandparents agree

36. Kids over twelve years old should not have to decide which parent they want to live with.

15% of single-parent kids agree   44% of parents agree
20% of stepparent kids agree   52% of grandparents agree

37. Parents should not have to wait a year or two after a divorce before dating other people.

79% of single-parent kids agree   72% of parents agree
72% of stepparent kids agree   67% of grandparents agree

38. Fathers should remarry so that the kids can have a mother.

3% of single-parent kids agree   0% of parents agree
5% of stepparent kids agree   5% of grandparents agree

39. Parents should stay together for the sake of the children.

23% of single-parent kids agree   11% of parents agree
11% of stepparent kids agree   38% of grandparents agree

40. A teenager should have the right to visit any grandparent
    or stepgrandparent during the year.

    81% of single-parent kids 94% of parents agree
          agree   100% of grandparents agree
        91% of stepparent kids agree

Sentence Completion

Included as part of the questionnaire are the following open-ended sentences. Try to complete each statement and then compare your answers with those of other kids about your age, which can be found on the pages that follow.

1.   Divorce is...

2.   Kids from divorced homes are...

3.   My experience with divorce is...

4. a. I believe in divorce because...
    b. I do not believe in divorce because...

5. People who get divorced are...

6. Teachers should understand that divorced kids are...

Sentence Completion Results

Some of the responses follow.

1. Divorce is . . .

"an interfamily feud with no one winning and the kids in the middle."

"a sad experience . . . it makes everyone very uncomfortable."

"hard at first, but after a while having divorced parents made me feel special. I get a lot of benefits."

"something kids should not have to go through."

"not a very pleasant thing in life, but some people just have to do it."

"harder on the kids than parents because the parents are getting away from the spouse they fight with but the children have to deal with who to live with, visit, when, etc."

"hard to talk to your parents about."

"a hard situation to experience, but you learn how to survive."

"a choice people must make if their home situation is very unpleasant or if they don't love each other."

"not as bad as people make it out to be. People overreact to it."

"good in a way if it relieves all the fighting and upset in a household."

"something that tears the love of the family apart and makes them do things that kids will worry about all their life."

"when people have changed or when the marriage was rushed into in the first place."

"good if parents don't feel the same way about each other."

"bad because you feel empty."

"when two people lose the love between them, they untie the knot and lead their lives in different directions."

2. Kids from divorced homes are . . .

"confused just like me and my parents."

"sometimes hard to understand. You don't know what they are going through."

"usually very depressed."

"just as normal on the outside but different inside."

"usually emotionally abused in some respect."

"emotional, touchy, angry, confused, very experienced travelers."

"lonely, depressed, angry."

"insecure. It really takes a lot out of them. It really hurts."

"probably more prepared for complicated situations in later life."

"more independent. When they depended on their parents, they got hurt badly by the divorce."

"very smart and can understand a lot of things."

"just like any other kid in school, sports, everything . . . except when they get home, they might have to go see their father or wash the dishes because he got the dishwasher."

"usually unhappy when divorce is new to them. They really, after a while, get used to it and resume a happy life."

"usually having troubles at home, school, and at friends' houses because they see everyone happy and really they're not."

"usually mean to others and don't care sometimes because of their feelings."

"a little different from others. They can be more independent, but they may have more pressures."

"really sweet. It seems like they understand you and your problems more than someone whose parents aren't divorced."

3. My experience with divorce is . . .

"not too good—it was very hard to get close to both parents."

"good—my parents have been divorced for about seven years, and they still are good friends. My mom is remarried, and I love my stepfather very much."

"that I was young when my parents got divorced, and I don't remember anything. But everyone gets along. The only thing is, we have to split up for the holidays."

"pretty bad because my parents still have big fights and it's all very confusing."

"that I can't always get the things I used to get."

"fun. Each day I have a new experience with my mom and dad."

"I think normal. I live with my mom and visit my father the first and third weekends of every month."

"fairly common. I live with my mom and my sister and visit my dad."

"that I have gotten more independent."

"my dad left my mom for some chick in Canada when I was in the fifth grade."

"was very difficult at first but now is much better."

"is good because I don't have to listen to fighting all the time."

"good, but I have become more dependent on myself and I learned you can only be hurt once by someone or something."

"I'm mad as hell and wish it never happened."

4. a. I believe in divorce because . . .

"if parents don't care about each other, it can wreck others' lives."

"if two people can't live together and be happy, they shouldn't have to be unhappy forever."

"if you don't get along together, there's no use being together."

"it's very hard on the kids if parents are living together and don't love each other."

"people do change, and they should have another chance to start over with someone else."

b. I do not believe in divorce because . . .

"my mother says it ruined her children's lives."

"people should be absolutely sure the person they're going to marry has habits and customs that you can live with."

"it's hard on the kids, and they shouldn't have gotten into something like that in the first place."

5. People who get divorced are . . .

"normal people; they just can't stay married to each other."

"doing what they think is best for themselves and their children."

"sometimes happier; sometimes sadder; sometimes don't care."

"mostly talking about their ex so and so because they still think of them."

"want to be with people their own age and need a sense of love."

"back stabbers."

"are usually taking it out on their kids and blaming their problems on other people."

"are really people who did not know the other person well. They did not know how it was going to be."

"much more responsible and independent."

"as human as anybody else."

"no different from anybody else except in the fact that they have been through a very bad experience they will never forget."

"just the same as other people, but now they're statistics."

6. Teachers should understand that divorced kids are...

"more troubled because they don't know what to expect one day from the other."

"don't need special privileges."

"very depressed."

"highly pressured at home."

"mad at the world and couldn't care less about their education."

"may do bad at their schoolwork."

"the same as other kids."

"under a lot of pressure."

"finding it difficult to concentrate on schoolwork."

"lonely."

"likely to come unprepared on Monday because they may have left stuff at the other parent's."

"probably in need of someone to talk to."

"normal. Just exactly the same as other kids."

"going through a lot, and all they want is someone to know what they are going through. Kids want someone to explain to them why it happens."

"people who want to be treated the same as anyone else. In sixth grade I took a class called 'Journal' in which I had to keep a diary of my feelings. The teacher read mine with me and began to cry because my home life was so ugly. She made me feel guilty."

More Sentence Completion

Very often if you are forced to put things on paper, your ideas become clearer and make more sense to you. Unless you have faithfully kept a journal, writing about what you feel is not easy, so the beginning of each sentence has been written for you. Think about yourself and how the divorce has affected you and then write in the *first* thought that comes to mind. Doing it will help you clarify some ideas, and reading it back later can also be enlightening.

Remember, write the first thing that comes to mind.

Complete the following sentences by writing the *first* thoughts that come to you.

1. I am really good at _____
_____

2. I worry about _____
_____

3. I like _____
_____

4. I get scared when _____
_____

5. I feel good when _____

6. It would be better if _____

7. I would like _____

8. My father and I _____

9. I miss _____

10. If my mother _____

11. I feel sorry _____

12. I get mad when _____

13. Parents should _____

14. I feel like _____

15. I am lucky because _____

16. It's my fault that _____

17. What bugs me is _____

18. When I'm with _____

19. My mother and I _____

_____

20. It's better now that _____

_____

Balance Sheet

With divorce, as in nearly every situation, there are at least two different ways of looking at it. Sometimes the good side is not as easy to see, but positive aspects do exist. Below is a balance sheet. In one column, record all the bad parts about your new life-style; and in the second column, record all the good things.

BAD	GOOD
___	___
___	___
___	___
___	___
___	___
___	___
___	___
___	___
___	___
___	___
___	___
___	___
___	___

About the Authors

JOHN P. BROGAN and LILA MAIDEN are both teachers at the Mildred E. Strang Middle School in Yorktown Heights, New York. They run a program called "Who Gets Me for Christmas?" that deals with separation, divorce, and remarriage. Both authors live in Westchester County, New York.